ANOREXIA AND BULIMIA
DANGEROUS EATING DISORDERS

By Kristen Rajczak Nelson

Portions of this book originally appeared in *Anorexia and Bulimia* by Elizabeth Silverthorne.

LUCENT PRESS

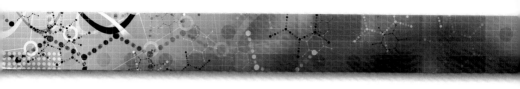

Published in 2020 by
Lucent Press, an Imprint of Greenhaven Publishing, LLC
353 3rd Avenue
Suite 255
New York, NY 10010

Designer: Deanna Paternostro
Editor: Jennifer Lombardo

Library of Congress Cataloging-in-Publication Data

Names: Rajczak Nelson, Kristen, author.
Title: Anorexia and bulimia : dangerous eating disorders / Kristen Rajczak
  Nelson.
Description: New York : Lucent Press, [2020] | Series: Diseases and disorders
  | Includes bibliographical references and index.
Identifiers: LCCN 2018048477 (print) | LCCN 2018049189 (ebook) | ISBN
  9781534567504 (eBook) | ISBN 9781534567498 (pbk. book) | ISBN
  9781534566934 (library bound book)
Subjects: LCSH: Anorexia nervosa–Popular works. | Bulimia–Popular works. |
  Eating disorders–Popular works. | Eating disorders–Treatment–Popular
  works.
Classification: LCC RC552.A5 (ebook) | LCC RC552.A5 R35 2020 (print) | DDC
  616.85/262–dc23
LC record available at https://lccn.loc.gov/2018048477

Printed in the United States of America

CPSIA compliance information: Batch #BS19KL: For further information contact Greenhaven Publishing LLC, New York, New York, at 1-844-317-7404.

Please visit our website, www.greenhavenpublishing.com. For a free color catalog of all our high-quality books, call toll free 1-844-317-7404 or fax 1-844-317-7405.

CONTENTS

Illness is an unfortunate part of life, and it is one that is often misunderstood. Thanks to advances in science and technology, people have been aware for many years that diseases such as the flu, pneumonia, and chickenpox are caused by viruses and bacteria. These diseases all cause physical symptoms that people can see and understand, and many people have dealt with these diseases themselves. However, sometimes diseases that were previously unknown in most of the world turn into epidemics and spread across the globe. Without an awareness of the method by which these diseases are spread—through the air, through human waste or fluids, through sexual contact, or by some other method—people cannot take the proper precautions to prevent further contamination. Panic often accompanies epidemics as a result of this lack of knowledge.

Knowledge is power in the case of mental disorders, as well. Mental disorders are just as common as physical disorders, but due to a lack of awareness among the general public, they are often stigmatized. Scientists have studied them for years and have found that they are generally caused by chemical imbalances in the brain, but they have not yet determined with certainty what causes those imbalances or how to fix them. Because even mild mental illness is stigmatized in Western society, many people prefer not to talk about it.

Chronic pain disorders are also not well understood—even by researchers—and do not yet have foolproof treatments. People who have a mental disorder or a disease or disorder that causes them to feel chronic pain can be the target of uninformed

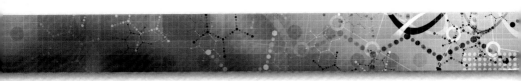

opinions. People who do not have these disorders sometimes struggle to understand how difficult it can be to deal with the symptoms. These disorders are often termed "invisible illnesses" because no one can see the symptoms; this leads many people to doubt that they exist or are serious problems. Additionally, people who have an undiagnosed disorder may understand that they are experiencing the world in a different way than their peers, but they have no one to turn to for answers.

Misinformation about all kinds of ailments is often spread through personal anecdotes, social media, and even news sources. This series aims to present accurate information about both physical and mental conditions so young adults will have a better understanding of them. Each volume discusses the symptoms of a particular disease or disorder, ways it is currently being treated, and the research that is being done to understand it further. Advice for people who may be suffering from a disorder is included, as well as information for their loved ones about how best to support them.

With fully cited quotes, a list of recommended books and websites for further research, and informational charts, this series provides young adults with a factual introduction to common illnesses. By learning more about these ailments, they will be better able to prevent the spread of contagious diseases, show compassion to people who are dealing with invisible illnesses, and take charge of their own health.

FIGHTING AGAINST YOUR BODY

Sit among a group of people having lunch, and observe the way they speak about their meal to one another. You might hear someone say, "I'll just have a salad. I'm trying to be good." Another person might chime in with, "I'm getting extra cheese on my burger and fries as my side. I already had a doughnut today, so who cares!" One person might endlessly proclaim how they could not possibly eat their entire meal. Still another might ask the waiter what the vegetables have been cooked in so she can count the meal's calories properly in her MyFitnessPal app.

Eating is something all people have to do to stay alive. It gives the body fuel to run properly and energy to take a walk, read a book, and hug family and friends. However, many people spend a lot of time preoccupied with what and how much they are eating. They are influenced by what their friends are eating, celebrity diets, and what they hear on talk shows. With so many people following different diets—such as WW, paleo, veganism, and keto—it can be hard to spot disordered eating. However, many of these "lifestyles" promote restricting certain foods and indulging in others, which can cause a person long-term psychological harm and can lead to physical problems. For many, the line between following these diets and developing an eating disorder is troublingly blurry. Over time, what can simply be called disordered eating—only eating at certain times of day, in strict quantities, or a few categories of food, for example—can worsen into a clinically diagnosable eating disorder.

Anorexia nervosa and bulimia nervosa are two major categories of these disorders. Characterized by behaviors that allow a person to eat as little as possible to achieve a low body weight, anorexia affects 0.9 percent of women in America during their lives. Behaviors of bulimia include eating large amounts of food followed by some kind of purging, either by abuse of laxatives (drugs that make a person have to go to the bathroom), excessive exercise, or vomiting. This disorder affects 1.5 percent of women in America at some point in their lives. These disorders are almost as common in men as they are in women, even though media coverage of male eating disorders has not been as common.

Eating is a necessary part of being human and should often be enjoyable. However, for almost 30 million Americans, it has become a life-threatening cycle of eating too much and vomiting, attempting to eat as little as possible, hours upon hours of exercise, and other destructive behaviors.

Coming Out

Eating disorders are not a creation of the 20th and 21st centuries, but it was not until about 40 years ago that they were recognized in the United States as a growing problem.

In 1979, Aimee Liu published *Solitaire*, a memoir about her struggles with an eating disorder that began when she was a teenager. She does not call herself a sufferer of anorexia because when she wrote the book at age 25, she did not know the name for her persistent eating issues. Her book was groundbreaking. It was one of the first narratives of this kind, telling the story of a teenage girl just trying to lose weight at first and the harmful obsession it became.

Then, in 1983, the world was shocked by the death of Karen Carpenter, the drummer and lead singer for the famous musical duo The Carpenters. She was only 32 years old at the time of her death and had been suffering from anorexia since her teen years after someone had told her she was chubby. Carpenter was the first celebrity to die of an eating disorder in the public eye. Although sad, her story had a positive outcome: Her struggles encouraged more celebrities to come forward with their own troubling stories.

Even knowing that other people were experiencing the same thing, it was still difficult for some to admit. After 17 years of dealing with bulimia, singer and dancer Paula Abdul—who later went on to be a judge on *American Idol*— spoke out about her eating disorder in 1995. As a professional cheerleader and dancer, the 5-foot 2-inch (1.5 m) tall Abdul had long felt pressure to compete with other taller, thinner dancers. Like

Paula Abdul stayed at a hospital for eating disorders for a month to begin her recovery. She told *People* magazine that her struggles inspired her music.

many, her struggles began when she was growing up. She has continued to raise awareness about eating disorders since.

Celebrities continue to come out to the public about their eating disorders today. Lady Gaga and Kesha have confirmed eating disorders in their pasts and have spoken about the trials of recovery. Singer Demi Lovato, who first underwent treatment for bulimia and anorexia in 2010, has been especially vocal about her continued struggles with food and exercise while continuing a career in entertainment.

In 2017, Demi Lovato said a breakup caused her to turn to eating disorder behaviors again.

Raising Awareness

While stories of celebrities shine a spotlight on eating disorders and recovery, these few brave, outspoken men and women are just a handful of those who deal with anorexia and bulimia every day. Most suffer quietly, just trying to get through their school day or workday without anyone noticing their disordered behaviors.

Understanding why a friend or family member might be turning to these behaviors can be difficult. It can seem like they are choosing to do themselves harm and that they could stop if they wanted to. However, it is important to know that the causes of anorexia and bulimia are varied, from family history to issues with anxiety and depression. Treatment for these illnesses can be lifelong, but with supportive, caring people around them, eating disorder sufferers have a greater chance of recovery. By learning the signs of eating disorder behavior, anyone could be the catalyst for someone realizing they need help and seeking it out.

Anorexia and bulimia can cause serious medical problems and may lead to death. From celebrity spokespeople to concerned friends, anyone who raises awareness about these conditions could save lives—even if it is just a comment about enjoying lunch instead of focusing on its calorie content.

EATING DISORDERS EXPLAINED

According to the National Eating Disorders Association (NEDA), eating disorders are "serious but treatable mental and physical illnesses that can affect people of every age, sex, gender, race, ethnicity, and socioeconomic group."[1] That means anyone can develop an eating disorder no matter who they are or what their family is like. When stated like that, it can sound scary, and it should. The mortality, or death, rates for eating disorders are some of the highest of any mental health disorder, with anorexia being the highest.

Since scientists and doctors do not know exactly what causes someone to develop an eating disorder, more research is being done every year to try to figure it out. Today, the reasons behind why some people develop an eating disorder and the medical community's view of these disorders are very different than they were in the past. This has also changed the public's view of those with eating disorders.

Eating Disorders Throughout History

Eating disorders as they are diagnosed and described today are modern disorders. However, the behaviors common to eating disorders have been recorded since the Middle Ages. For example, the wealthy of this time would engage in vomiting after eating a large meal so they could eat even more. This was referenced in a scene in the popular movie and book series *The Hunger Games*, when a party at the wealthy Capitol served a vomit-inducing liquid alongside the food.

Self-starvation practices have been traced to religious beliefs during the Middle Ages. Hermits of the Christian faith would refuse to eat in an attempt to achieve spiritual purity, and Saint Jerome preached the benefits of this lifestyle choice. However, most of the time, records of food restriction and self-starvation have been linked to

Some scholars believe Catherine of Siena may have begun her fasting practices to avoid a marriage her parents were trying to arrange for her.

women. These women were trying to become closer to God by denying themselves food, but this often led to death. Saint Catherine of Siena was one such casualty. She lived from 1347 to 1380 and was well known for eating very little for long periods of time. She and others believed they could prove how devoted they were to God by doing so. Behaviors of fasting for long periods for religious reasons have been called "holy anorexia" by some authors.

During the Renaissance, the reasons for self-starvation behaviors began to shift away from the religious. Material reasons began to become part of the equation as beauty ideals shifted. In the past, a heavier body type was considered beautiful, but over time, slimness became the ideal. By the late 1770s, medical and psychological reasons for this behavior began to be discussed, though it was still described by some as possibly being caused by an "ill and morbid state of the spirits."[2]

By the 1800s, medical professionals were observing and writing about a variety of cases of self-starvation and other disordered eating behaviors. The first medical paper that tried to describe these behaviors came out in 1860. Not long after, Sir William Gull called collections of behaviors like this "anorexia nervosa." Previously, a person who showed such behavior might be considered to have "hysteria," but Gull saw a separate disorder. He said it could happen in both men and women. His work and that of others made it clear they were considering the disorder psychological. The late 1880s brought more descriptions of disordered eating behaviors. By the early 1900s, behaviors that are now associated with bulimia nervosa were also being noted.

Early Cause Theories

Today, medical professionals know eating disorders have multiple complex causes, and there is still much to learn about how they come about in an individual. However, in the past, many theories were considered in the search for the cause of and cure for disordered eating behaviors.

Disordered eating behavior after the Middle Ages was sometimes considered religious hysteria. Other times, it was thought to be a biological eating problem. One theory considered it a problem with the endocrine system, which regulates the body's hormones. Eating disorders were believed to have been caused by an imbalance of a person's hormones or a problem with the pituitary gland, which controls most of the other glands in the endocrine system. Another belief was that a person's parents or family caused their eating disorder. For a long time, those with anorexia may have been treated for their disorder by being removed from their parents. Anorexia was even thought to be a form of the disease tuberculosis or to have a sexual origin.

The Modern Era

In 1952, the American Psychological Association (APA) released the first *Diagnostic and Statistical Manual* (*DSM-I*), a listing of all recognized mental health disorders that included diagnostic criteria and descriptions. This manual included one eating disorder: anorexia nervosa. In 1968, the second edition (*DSM-II*) moved the disorder to a grouping called special symptoms/feeding disturbances. This grouping also included pica, a disorder characterized by a desire to eat non-food items, and rumination, a disorder characterized by a person regurgitating food to chew it again.

The 1970s proved to be a turning point in the history of eating disorders. At this time, medical professionals were seeing a rise in both anorexia and the behaviors associated with bulimia, as well as a rise in obesity. Important books and articles about eating disorders were published, including Dr. Hilde Bruch's *Eating Disorders: Obesity, Anorexia Nervosa, and the Person Within*.

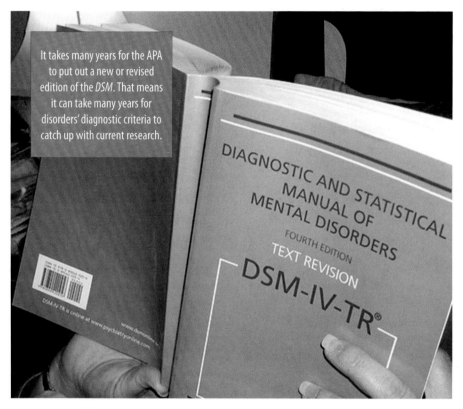

It takes many years for the APA to put out a new or revised edition of the *DSM*. That means it can take many years for disorders' diagnostic criteria to catch up with current research.

The first major paper discussing cases of bulimia came out too. Gerard Russell, a British psychologist, had begun noting differences between anorexia and another distinct eating disorder in 1972 when he met a woman who came to him for anorexia treatment but did not present with the signs of anorexia. After several years of observing other similar cases, he published "Bulimia Nervosa: An Ominous Variant of Anorexia Nervosa" in 1979, including the differences between patients with anorexia and the now-named bulimia.

When the *DSM-III* came out in 1980, a section focusing solely on eating disorders was added. This edition of the *DSM*, which arrived in 1987, included bulimia as its own category under the heading of eating disorders. By then, the death of Karen Carpenter and other celebrity confessions of eating disorders had brought them into the public consciousness and given them greater prevalence in the psychiatric community.

Since then, the diagnostic criteria have only become more refined with each edition and revision of the *DSM* as medical professionals learn more about why some people develop anorexia and bulimia, the signs of these disorders, and proper treatments.

There are three main classifications of eating disorders used by medical professionals today: anorexia nervosa, bulimia nervosa, and binge eating disorder (BED). These are listed in the fifth edition of the *DSM* under the broader category of feeding and eating disorders, which again lists them alongside feeding disorders such as pica and rumination.

Anorexia

Someone who suffers from anorexia worries a lot about how their body looks and manages their food intake with that in mind. They typically try to lose weight by severely limiting the amount of food they eat. They may skip meals and lie about having eaten. When they eat with others, they may move food around on their plate without eating it, or they may hide some of it in their napkin to throw out later. They may take a very long time to eat very little. For example, one person with anorexia described taking an hour to eat her meal, which consisted only of one apple. Another told how she divided a cookie into 32 sections to eat over several days. Another way people with anorexia lose weight is through excessive, compulsive exercise. The weight loss associated with these behaviors becomes the most important part of their self-esteem.

Someone with anorexia has not lost their appetite. They are simply ignoring it.

Anorexia means "loss of appetite," but that is not what actually happens to someone suffering from anorexia. In fact, when many people with anorexia first begin to restrict their food, they may be very hungry. Instead of fulfilling their needs, they ignore them by simply refusing to eat.

The *DSM* includes two types of anorexia: restricting and binge eating/purging. Those who are considered restricting type keep the calories they take in very low by restricting their food

Binge Eating Disorder

The word "binge" is often used to describe excess drinking or consuming a large amount of something, such as a TV show, in a short amount of time. Sometimes, people who occasionally eat more than normal might say they "binged" on ice cream or potato chips. When eating disorder experts use the term "binge," they are generally referring to eating a large amount of food in combination with a feeling of loss of control or dissociation, which is a feeling of being disconnected from a person's own thoughts or actions.

Christopher G. Fairburn, a specialist in treating binge eating disorder, described the aftermath of a binge:

> Those who binge may say they experience some immediate, though temporary positive feelings. For example, they may feel a sense of relief. Feelings of hunger and deprivation will have disappeared, and perhaps the depression or anxiety that may have triggered the binge has been displaced. But these positive effects are soon replaced by feelings of shame, disgust, and guilt.[1]

Like anorexia and bulimia, binge eating disorder (BED) is dangerous. People who binge characteristically eat large quantities of food in short periods of time, eat when not hungry, eat in secret, and feel distress and guilt over their behavior despite feeling unable to control it. For a long time, it was known as compulsive overeating. In early editions of the *DSM*, binge eating was mentioned as a sign of bulimia. In 2013, BED was listed as a separate category from bulimia in the *DSM-5*.

Not all binge eaters are overweight. Some, however, become seriously obese—a condition that can lead to life-threatening health problems. These health risks are similar to those associated with clinical obesity and, according to the Eating Recovery Center, include:

- *High blood pressure*
- *High cholesterol*
- *Heart disease*
- *Type II diabetes mellitus*[2]

1. Christopher G. Fairburn, *Overcoming Binge Eating*. New York, NY: Guilford, 1995, p. 20.

2. "Binge Eating Disorder (BED) Health Risks," Eating Recovery Center, accessed on September 28, 2018. www.eatingrecoverycenter.com/conditions/binge-eating/health-risks.

and may exercise excessively. Someone with the binge eating/purge type of anorexia also restricts food taken in but also may self-induce vomiting or use laxatives, diuretics, or enemas to cause them to go to the bathroom more frequently than normal so they can get the food they eat out of their system before their body can absorb it. This prevents them from absorbing the calories in the food, but it also prevents them from absorbing essential nutrients.

Bulimia

The signs of bulimia are often not as apparent as those of anorexia. Similar to anorexia, a person with bulimia gets their sense of self-worth from what they think of their body shape or size. The term bulimia comes from Greek words meaning "ox-hunger." That is a good description because people with bulimia typically eat large amounts of food whether they are hungry or not.

People with bulimia may be of normal weight or slightly overweight. It is not obvious from looking at them that they are obsessed with their body weight and shape. Those with bulimia typically eat much more than standard food portions. This might be a whole cake instead of a slice, or a box of cookies instead of just a few. Then, filled with horror at the idea of gaining weight, they engage in vomiting or misuse laxatives, diuretics, or enemas to purge the food from their bodies. They may also excessively exercise, fast, or misuse medication. Because their behavior takes place in secret and their appearance changes less than that of someone with anorexia, sufferers of bulimia are often able to hide their disease for years. Bulimia is differentiated from the binge eating/purging type of anorexia because those with this type of anorexia cannot maintain a normal weight, while those with bulimia often do.

Who Suffers?

The National Institute of Mental Health (NIMH) lists anorexia nervosa and bulimia nervosa as the two deadliest eating disorders. Eating disorder victims often try to hide their disease or claim their symptoms (such as extreme thinness) arise from some other cause. This behavior makes it impossible to know exactly how many people are suffering from eating disorders, at what age they first developed symptoms, or how they are being affected by them. Data from reliable sources, however, shows that despite growing awareness of the seriousness of these diseases, the number of victims is increasing. In fact, experts agree that eating disorders have reached epidemic levels in America, and many segments of the population are truly at risk. As the NEDA reported, "National surveys estimate that 20 million women and 10 million men in America will have an eating disorder at some point in their lives."[3]

According to the Cleveland Clinic, both anorexia and bulimia most often begin occurring in adolescence. However, children under age 12 can also suffer from these eating disorders. The number of sufferers in this age group has been on the rise since the 1990s and includes both boys and girls. However, the largest group found to be diagnosed with any eating disorder, including anorexia and bulimia, are women between the ages of 12 and 35.

The places with the highest numbers of eating disorders are the United States, Europe, Canada, South Africa, and New Zealand. All of these are industrialized societies that have more than enough food and idealize thinness. Some ethnic groups in the United States are more likely to develop eating disorders, such as Latina, Native American, and African American women. None of these groups have as high a number of people with eating disorders as the white population, but people of color in general are at high risk of developing eating disorders. The NEDA reported that black teens have a 50-percent greater chance of bingeing and purging than white teens. A study has also shown that those who are Latinx have also been found to be more likely to suffer from bulimia than non-Latinx adolescents. Socioeconomic status may also play a role in who develops eating disorders. The NEDA reported that teen girls from low-income families are 153 percent more likely to develop an eating disorder. All of this

It is sometimes difficult to tell whether someone has an eating disorder by how they look. Similarly, it is difficult to tell who is at risk for developing an eating disorder simply by their sex, age, or skin color.

data debunks the common belief that anorexia and bulimia are found most often in upper class, white, teenage women.

Anorexia Among the Black Population

Sufferers of anorexia who are black may be more common than statistics show, according to reporter Shannah Tharp-Taylor. In 2003, she wrote,

Black women often suffer needlessly from anorexia because doctors do not expect to find eating disorders in the African American community and thus misdiagnose their anorexic patients. It has been thought that the African American community's greater acceptance of larger body sizes for women offers black teens some protection against anorexia. However, as African Americans take on the cultural values of the mainstream — white — culture, any protection provided by greater acceptance of diverse body types has diminished. While more research on eating disorders in minorities is needed, it appears that anorexia depends more on socioeconomic status than on race.[1]

1. Shannah Tharp-Taylor, "Anorexia Among Black Women Gets New Scrutiny," *Chicago Tribune*, August 25, 2003, p. 1.

Additionally, though more women overall suffer from eating disorders, a significant number of men deal with anorexia, bulimia, and other eating disorders. In the United States, about one-third of the 30 million people who develop an eating disorder in their lifetime are men. According to the NEDA, men represent about 25 percent of all cases of those with anorexia and 25 percent of those with bulimia. Between 1999 and 2009, male eating disorder hospitalization increased by more than 50 percent. Former professional baseball player Mike Marjama retired from the Seattle Mariners in 2018 to work with the NEDA. He believes more attention needs to be focused on the large number of men who suffer from eating disorders. Marjama said, "There are men who have

Mike Marjama achieved his dream of playing in the major leagues. His new goal is to bring awareness to men with eating disorders.

told me they've suffered with this illness for 30 or 40 years and felt like they haven't been able to say anything about it."[4]

A 2007 study found that gay and bisexual men represent a disproportionate number of male eating disorders. Although only about 5 percent of the total population of men identify as gay, about 42 percent of men with eating disorders identify as gay. Another study found that gay men were 12 times more likely to purge than men who identified as heterosexual. Those who identify as transgender also have much higher rates of eating disorders than people who do not identify as transgender.

Regardless of a sufferer's age, sex, gender, sexual orientation, or ethnic background, anorexia and

Studies show that women who identify as lesbians have less body dissatisfaction than heterosexual women. However, it seems there is not a big difference between lesbian or bisexual women and heterosexual women in the prevalence of eating disorders.

bulimia are serious illnesses. They often present in certain ways that may tip off family members, friends, and doctors to a person's troubling eating behaviors.

CHAPTER TWO

WARNING SIGNS

When comedian Whitney Cummings was about 11 years old, she started restricting her food choices. She would eat just one kind of food for a month and obsessively controlled her intake. This continued throughout her teen years and into her 20s, when she also started bingeing and over-exercising. For years, she truly did not see that her behavior was a problem. Then, in her late 20s, her hair started falling out. Cummings would get horrible migraines. Suddenly, the pieces began to come together: She needed to stop and get help.

Cummings's story shares many elements with others fighting with their bodies to look a certain way. These behaviors can develop into full-blown anorexia and bulimia quietly because many who suffer from eating disorders deny that anything is wrong. These actions often happen in secret. Additionally, because exercising and dieting are so accepted in American culture—particularly in the entertainment industry Cummings was navigating—it may take family and friends a long time to notice that someone has crossed the line into an eating disorder.

However, there are many signs of both anorexia and bulimia that can be recognized. These are often used in diagnosis—the formal, medical acknowl-edgement that someone is experiencing a problem that needs treatment. Knowing these signs could save someone's life.

Whitney Cummings is the creator of the TV show *2 Broke Girls*. She also wrote and appeared on her own series, *Whitney*.

Anorexia: Warning Signs and Behaviors

At first, it might not be obvious that someone is suffering from anorexia. They may simply say they are trying to lose weight. They may say their appetite is normal and that they are hungry. However, friends and family may notice comments about "feeling fat" or other statements showing low self-esteem, poor body image, and a lack of understanding that their body has become smaller. Those with anorexia may obsessively weigh themselves, and as they lose more and more weight, it can become apparent to those around them that they are not eating much.

According to the NIMH, some warning signs of developing anorexia include:

- *Extremely restricted eating*

- *Extreme thinness (emaciation)*

- *A relentless pursuit of thinness and unwillingness to maintain a normal or healthy weight*

- *Intense fear of gaining weight*

- *Distorted body image, a self-esteem that is heavily influenced by perceptions of body weight and shape, or a denial of the seriousness of low body weight* [5]

Another behavior someone battling anorexia may engage in is excessive exercise. They may begin running farther and farther distances in an effort to burn extra calories, visit the gym more than once a day, or take hours of exercise classes in a row. From the outside, this can look like a newly adopted fitness habit, but those with anorexia take their fitness too far.

In addition to causing mental distress, excessive exercise can add to the physical problems someone with anorexia faces. Girls who exercise too much may change their menstrual cycle or cause it to stop entirely. In *The Truth About Eating Disorders*, Gerri Kramer wrote, "People who exercise compulsively may experience dehydration, broken bones, torn ligaments, joint problems, osteoporosis, and even heart and kidney failure. A healthy amount of exercise builds muscle, but too much actually destroys the muscle."[6]

If a strenuous exercise routine is interfering with other aspects of life, it has likely become a problem that may need clinical help.

In addition to overexercising, someone with anorexia may take diet pills or laxatives and may even throw up after they eat.

The Mayo Clinic lists a number of behavioral warning signs that someone is developing or has developed an eating disorder such as anorexia, including:

- *Skipping meals or making excuses for not eating*

- *Adopting an overly restrictive vegetarian diet*

- *Excessive focus on healthy eating*

- *Making own meals rather than eating what the family eats*

- *Withdrawing from normal social activities*

- *Persistent worry or complaining about being fat and talk of losing weight*

How Much Exercise Is Too Much?

For most people, taking part in exercise every day or several times a week is healthy. Some people enjoy training for long-distance cycling or running events. Others want to see how much weight they can lift. Most just want to keep their body healthy. However, for someone with an eating disorder, exercise is just one more way to deprive their body of needed calories. Their food and workout become parts of a transactional relationship—the more they eat, the more they need to move. They may also add more exercise to their routine because they find their food restriction unsustainable. Writer and eating disorder advocate Tabitha Farrar wrote on her blog that when she was going through anorexia, her doctor never asked how much she was exercising, only how much she was eating: "I *was* eating, but that was on the condition that I exercised for over six hours a day. In a sense, my Anorexia was hiding in plain sight."[1]

She described the intense fear she felt from not being able to exercise as much as she felt she needed to. Farrar recalled that her need to negate calories extended even beyond formal exercise:

> The compulsion to move continued to exist in practically every move I made. Taking the longer route. Walking rather than taking the car. Getting up and down to fetch things when eating a meal. Never sitting. Always having to stand. Fidgeting. I was not allowed to sit down during the day. If I had to (say a car ride or a situation where I could not stand) I would have to "make it right" by eating less that day.[2]

After realizing she needed to stop exercising to get well, it took Farrar two years to actually stop. She acknowledges that the role exercise played in her anorexia was the hardest part for her to overcome. For her, the only way to stop the excessive exercise cycle was to quit "cold turkey," or all at once—something she recommends to others facing a similar struggle.

1. Tabitha Farrar, "Exercise and Anorexia: The Case for Cold Turkey," Tabitha Farrar, May 2017. tabithafarrar.com/2017/05/exercise-anorexia-case-cold-turkey/.

2. Farrar, "Exercise and Anorexia."

- *Frequent checking in the mirror for perceived flaws*

- *Expressing depression, disgust, shame or guilt about eating habits*

- *Eating in secret* [7]

These behaviors may only be obvious to a friend or family member who is specifically on the look-out for warning signs, especially since many people with anorexia try to engage in their behavior without anyone knowing. Over time, though, physical symptoms of anorexia arise. A very low body weight is one obvious symptom, although some people may try to hide this by wearing layers of clothing or baggy clothing. Someone with anorexia may complain about being very tired, cold, or constipated. Their skin can take on a yellowish color and begin to look dry. Their hair and nails will become brittle and break easily. Some people with anorexia grow fine hairs all over their body called lanugo. The body does this to try to keep its temperature up in the absence of calories to burn for heat. These are only the physical problems that can be seen; less visible, internal medical issues are also caused by anorexia.

Bulimia: Warning Signs and Behaviors

Actress Candace Cameron Bure did not struggle with disordered eating until she was an adult. When she married her husband, a professional hockey player, she moved away from all her family and friends. She said she lost a sense of who she was:

> *I sat lonely so many nights not knowing what to do with myself. But there was always one friend that was always there, that was so readily available anytime I wanted, and that for me was food … It became a very destructive relationship, and it was one that really caught me off guard. I got into a cycle of binge eating and feeling such guilt and shame for that, that I would start purging. And without even knowing, it soon just took over to a point where you feel such a loss of control.*[8]

Her father eventually found out about her behavior, and Bure was able to stop. However, a few years later, she started bingeing and purging again. This time, she got professional help and has successfully recovered.

Like anorexia, the behaviors that are signs of bulimia often happen in secret and are accompanied by feelings of shame. Binge eating behaviors, such as those Bure described, might only happen when a person is alone. They can be triggered in someone with bulimia by a stressful situation, feeling hunger after trying to restrict food intake,

Candace Cameron Bure is best known for playing D.J. Tanner on *Full House* and D.J. Fuller on *Fuller House*.

or feeling badly about one's self and body shape. Following a binge, someone with bulimia will force themselves to purge the calories they have taken in by throwing up, taking many laxatives, fasting, or exercising excessively. It is important to remember that bulimia and binge eating disorder share the component of a binge, but in BED, the sufferer will not engage in purging behavior on a regular basis like someone with bulimia.

Bulimia can be hard for friends and family to spot for a significant reason: Many of those suffering from bulimia are a normal or healthy weight or even a bit overweight. Since those with bulimia, like those with many eating disorders, are striving for a certain look for their body, this often causes the disorder to continue. This makes the binge eating/purging type of anorexia different from bulimia, too, since those with that type of anorexia will not be able to maintain a normal weight.

Sometimes it is a dentist who first notices some of the telltale signs of bulimia, such as damaged teeth and gums. When a person vomits frequently, stomach acid wears away the enamel of their teeth and causes them to turn brown. Frequent vomiting also causes sores in the throat and mouth. It may cause swelling of the salivary glands in the cheeks (a condition commonly called "chipmunk cheeks"), and the voice of the person with chronic bulimia may become hoarse. Another clue to behaviors of someone with bulimia is the appearance of bruises, sores, or calluses on the knuckles or fingers. These occur when the person sticks their fingers down their throat to make themselves vomit and the fingers scrape against the teeth.

Friends and family can watch for some warning signs that a loved one might be suffering from bulimia in addition to calluses or sores on hands and a hoarse voice. They may hear someone suffering from bulimia be overly critical of their body shape and weight. According to the website Eating Disorder Hope, those who have developed bulimia may isolate themselves and tend to eat in private. They may hide food. Most obviously, someone suffering from bulimia will often go to the bathroom during a meal or right after they have eaten.

The NEDA lists several more warning signs of bulimia:

- *In general, behaviors and attitudes indicate that weight loss, dieting, and control of food are becoming primary concerns*

- *Evidence of binge eating, including disappearance of large amounts of food in short periods of time or lots of empty wrappers and containers indicating consumption of large amounts of food*

- *Evidence of purging behaviors, including frequent trips to the bathroom after meals, signs and/or smells of vomiting, presence of wrappers or packages of laxatives or diuretics*

- *Appears uncomfortable eating around others*

- *Develops food rituals (e.g. eats only a particular food or food group [e.g. condiments], excessive chewing, doesn't allow foods to touch)*

- *Skips meals or takes small portions of food at regular meals*

- *Any new practice with food or fad diets, including cutting out entire food groups (no sugar, no carbs, no dairy, vegetarianism/veganism)*

- *Fear of eating in public or with others*

- *Steals or hoards food in strange places*

- *Drinks excessive amounts of water or non-caloric beverages*

- *Uses excessive amounts of mouthwash, mints, and gum*

- *Maintains excessive, rigid exercise regimen—despite weather, fatigue, illness, or injury—due to the need to "burn off" calories*

- *Creates lifestyle schedules or rituals to make time for binge-and-purge sessions*

- *Withdraws from usual friends and activities*

- *Looks bloated from fluid retention*

- *Extreme mood swings*[9]

A Biological Reason

The rituals and secrecy of the behaviors of anorexia and bulimia may sound exhausting to someone not dealing with these disorders. However, there is evidence that these behaviors make sufferers feel good temporarily. Some medical professionals believe those who purge may experience a rush of endorphins, which are the feel-good hormones the body creates.

As the warning signs show, many behaviors and warning signs of anorexia and bulimia are similar. Additionally, according to the testimony of many medical experts, incidences of anorexia and bulimia are frequently interlinked; for instance, a patient with bulimia often has a history of anorexia. When the anorexia is supposedly cured, the eating disorder sometimes reemerges as bulimia. This means someone with an eating disorder may receive several diagnoses, as their behavior may be consistent with multiple disorders.

Portia de Rossi

When Portia de Rossi was 12 years old, her modeling agents told her to go on a diet, so she did not eat for 10 days. This began a terrible cycle that would end with her sick and hospitalized, causing her family and friends constant worry.

De Rossi revealed her history of anorexia and bulimia in her 2010 book, *Unbearable Lightness: A Story of Loss and Gain*. In it, she tells of dieting throughout her teens to stay thin, fearful that if she did not, she would not get work as a model anymore. As she continued to work in the entertainment industry, her eating behaviors remained unpredictable, especially as she struggled to conceal a second secret: the fact that she was a lesbian.

Unbearable Lightness includes a deep look into the mind of a woman in the depths of disorder, including details about eating in her car and throwing up on the side of the road so her brother would not find out what she was doing. It includes the incredibly low levels of calories she would eat, followed by uncontrollable binges, all in an effort to achieve a certain look. She wrote of her struggle with the positive attention her weight loss gained her as well as how dependent her mood was on her weight:

> Lying in bed Christmas morning, I felt thin. I could feel my hip bones and my ribs. I felt as though I could get on that scale and give myself the Christmas present of a good number, a number that would congratulate me for dieting successfully for eight months. The number would determine whether I had a happy Christmas or a miserable one.[1]

De Rossi's book reveals much about what it is like to have an eating disorder, but it would not be an appropriate book for someone in recovery to read, since it could trigger the renewal of symptoms.

Today, Portia de Rossi says that she accepts herself as she is and believes women should focus more on developing their mind and career and worry less about their body.

1. Quoted in Julie Jordan, "Portia De Rossi's Anorexia Battle: Lucky to Be Alive," *People*, November 15, 2010. people.com/archive/cover-story-portia-de-rossis-anorexia-battle-lucky-to-be-alive-vol-74-no-18/.

Are Men Different?

When anorexia and bulimia are developing, it can be very difficult for loved ones to notice that their friend or family member is engaging in disordered behaviors. Spotting warning signs of an eating disorder may be even more difficult if the sufferer is male. This is likely due to the societal assumption that people with anorexia and bulimia are female. Although it is true that many people with eating disorders are women, men can also have a poor body image that they try to combat with the behaviors associated with anorexia and bulimia. The essential features of eating disorders are the same regardless of a person's gender. Still, there are some warning signs that tend to be unique to male sufferers.

First, men may use excessive exercise for other reasons than to lose weight, although some also use it for that. They may develop an unhealthy obsession with gaining muscle mass—getting "shredded" or "ripped"—or with becoming a better athlete. All of this may be partly to attain a certain body type that society tells them is the "ideal," just like the women who excessively exercise and diet. The body type just happens to be big and muscular rather than small and slim. A clear obsession with "getting big" can be a warning sign that a man is developing anorexia or bulimia. Sometimes, these behaviors are called "bigorexia," although this is not a medical term.

Another warning sign is even harder to detect. Men dealing with an eating disorder also control their food intake and sometimes try to eat less and less. Others may be incredibly focused on the kinds of foods they are eating and make a strict plan for their intake, often including a lot of protein for muscle-building purposes.

Zayn Malik has said that when he was touring with One Direction, he would skip many meals—sometimes for days. He now recognizes that he was suffering from an eating disorder.

Male disordered eating behaviors can sometimes provide clear warning signs that something is wrong, but they tend to be explained away by practices that are culturally acceptable. For example, binge eating can affect men, though they may be praised for the amount of food they can eat. According to the American Addictions Centers, "Some people believe that men, if given the opportunity, will sit down and eat everything they can find. This is a cultural expectation, and it makes

Mike Marjama

Former Major League Baseball (MLB) catcher Mike Marjama recognizes his perfectionist tendencies. He speaks about his great work ethic and the pride he has in that. However, in his early teens, Marjama's perfectionism was put to work on a pursuit that soon became a risk to his health: losing weight. He said, "When I do a school project, it was done perfect. When I need something done, I write a paper, it's done perfect. When it comes to not eating, I did it perfect … My inner desire to be perfect is either my best friend or it's my worst enemy."[1]

From junior high into high school, Marjama worked to eat less and work out more. He did not think anything was wrong with his behavior, even though he did things such as putting a stationary bike in the bathroom, wearing sweats, and turning the shower to hot so he could cycle in the steam until he almost felt like he was going to pass out.

No one noticed his problematic behavior for a long time. Then, at one family dinner, he ate barely anything, and his mother finally saw what was happening. He was sent to a personal trainer who advised him to eat more; instead, he ate less. His family sent him to see a counselor, but he was resistant to changing his ways. When he showed up for a session having lost 14 pounds over 4 days, it was not up to him anymore. An ambulance was called, and he was hospitalized.

Marjama missed his junior year season of baseball in high school while he went through treatment for his eating disorder. Treatment was difficult, partly because he was the only young man among a group of young women at the hospital. Today, he says that a man, much less a professional athlete, speaking out about an eating disorder is still rare—but it is important. Marjama felt so strongly about the cause that after many years in the minor leagues and a short time with the Seattle Mariners, he retired from baseball to work with the NEDA full time.

1. "Mike Marjama Overcomes Eating Disorder on Path to MLB," YouTube video, 7:27, posted by UNINTERRUPTED, March 28, 2018. www.youtube.com/watch?v=awlLNvTH6PA.

[bingeing] at least familiar, if not accepted, behavior for all men."[10] Men might believe the opposite to be true too:

> If it is assumed that lazy, unappealing men eat anything they can eat in great amounts, men with anorexia or bulimia who have very strict rules about what they can and cannot eat might be praised for that behavior. It might seem as though they are pushing back against a negative stereotype,

and they might get recognition, not concern, for the food choices they make.[11]

Excessive workout behavior is also more accepted for men than for women, as society's expectations for men revolve around being strong.

Because of these cultural ideas, men are less likely to have someone notice their behavior. Like those around them, they may not even see their behaviors as disordered. However, their body dissatisfaction is consistent with anyone who has anorexia or bulimia. It can have an incredibly negative effect on their overall mental health:

> *If he cannot talk about the way he feels about his body, or if he does not feel as though he can discuss the foods he either craves or ignores, even though these are thoughts that consume him, he may not feel as though he can have an authentic relationship. He may withdraw from his relationships altogether, or he may lash out at the few people who are trying to help him. As his isolation grows, his need to medicate with food may grow yet stronger.*[12]

Understanding warning signs can help those with anorexia and bulimia recognize they need help or can cause those around them to see that help should be offered. Regardless of whether someone is male or female, warning signs should not be ignored. They are crucial to notice for diagnosis to occur and treatment to follow.

Many people with anorexia and bulimia only receive treatment for their eating disorder after being formally diagnosed with it by a doctor. A patient must meet the criteria listed in the *DSM-5* in order to be given such a diagnosis.

DSM–5 Diagnostic Criteria for Anorexia Nervosa

Diagnostic criteria are conditions that must be present for someone to be diagnosed with a disorder. They are extremely important because some disorders look similar to each other and because sometimes people show certain symptoms of a disorder without actually having it. For example, if someone is traveling a long distance and does not have enough money to buy food at the airport, they may not eat a lot that day, but this does not mean they have anorexia. The diagnostic criteria for anorexia are:

> A. *Restriction of energy intake relative to requirements, leading to a significantly low body weight in the context of age, sex, developmental trajectory, and physical health. Significantly low weight is defined as a weight that is less than minimally normal or, for children and adolescents, less than that minimally expected.*

> B. *Intense fear of gaining weight or of becoming fat, or persistent behavior that interferes with weight gain, even though at a significantly low weight.*

> C. *Disturbance in the way in which one's body weight or shape is experienced, undue influence of body weight or shape on self-evaluation, or persistent lack of recognition of the seriousness of the current low body weight.*[13]

To be diagnosed with restricting type anorexia, a person must not have binged or purged in at least three months; instead, they must have achieved their unusually low weight "primarily through dieting, fasting, and/or excessive exercise."[14] To be diagnosed with binge eating/purging type, the person must have engaged in more than one episode of this behavior.

To diagnose the severity of a person's anorexia, doctors take into account how far below the typical body mass index (BMI) a person is. BMI is a measure of body fat based on a calculation of the person's height and weight. While it is not completely accurate for every individual, it is a useful way for doctors to determine how far below a healthy weight a person with anorexia is.

DSM-5 Diagnostic Criteria for Bulimia Nervosa

People with bulimia regularly engage in episodes of binge eating. This is defined as:

> *1. Eating, in a discrete period of time (e.g., within any 2-hour period), an amount of food that is definitely larger than what most individuals would eat in a similar period of time under similar circumstances.*

> *2. A sense of lack of control over eating during the episode (e.g., a feeling that one cannot stop eating or control what or how much one is eating).*[15]

After binge eating, people with bulimia compensate for the large amount of food they have consumed by purging. This is an important part of the diagnosis because it distinguishes bulimia from BED. Furthermore, to diagnose bulimia, the bingeing and purging must occur together at least once a week for three months, and the person must be excessively concerned about their body image. To distinguish bulimia from binge eating/purging type anorexia, bulimic behaviors must not "occur exclusively during episodes of anorexia nervosa."[16]

Because people with bulimia tend to maintain a

more average body weight than people with anorexia, the criteria for determining severity is different. Instead of going by BMI, the severity of bulimia is judged by the number of times a person purges per week. For example, a mild case involves one to three episodes of purging per week, while an extreme case involves 14 or more per week. However, when determining the level of severity, doctors may also take into account how much the symptoms of the disorder affect the person's life.

Recent *DSM* Updates

Since the first edition of the *DSM* was published, the diagnostic categories and criteria for many mental health issues, including eating disorders, have changed. In the most recent edition, the *DSM-5*, some significant updates to the eating disorder criteria were made. Previously, amenorrhea, or the loss of the menstrual cycle, was a criterion for anorexia nervosa. This has been removed, allowing the diagnosis to be more inclusive. Since everyone's body is different, some women keep having a period even when they lose a lot of weight. Before the change to the diagnostic criteria, these women could not be diagnosed with anorexia even if they had all the other symptoms. The removal of amenorrhea from the criteria also makes the diagnosis more inclusive of men who never had a period to begin with. No longer is there a weight requirement for an anorexia diagnosis either. Instead, the *DSM-5* asks that health care professionals evaluate a person's weight in the context of their age, health, sex, and overall development.

The criteria for bulimia nervosa also changed slightly from older *DSM* versions. First, the required frequency of purge behavior for diagnosis changed to once a week for three months instead of twice a week for three months. It also eliminated subtypes of bulimia. In addition, BED became a separate disorder with its own criteria for diagnosis.

Some people wonder why diseases and disorders need to have labels. Having a diagnosable mental health issue that is included in the *DSM* can help sufferers get all or part of their treatment paid for by their health insurance.

These changes were made to make the criteria easier for doctors and other health care professionals to understand and use. They were also meant to decrease the number of patients diagnosed with less specific eating disorders.

Rating Tests

Doctors and other medical professionals spend time ruling out other illnesses or disorders that could affect a person's weight, physical health, and mental health before someone is given a diagnosis of an eating disorder. For example, patients with hyperthyroidism can have weight loss, amenorrhea, or problems absorbing food—but they do not have dis-ordered eating behavior. In these cases, the patient's symptoms are caused when their thyroid gland, which plays a role in regulating weight, does not function as it should. In order to determine whether someone meets the criteria of the *DSM*, doctors often interview their patients showing symptoms of anorexia or bulimia. They may also use rating tests such as the Eating Attitudes Test, Eating Disorders Inventory, or Body Shape Questionnaire to aid in a confident diagnosis. The answers to the questions on these rating tools are self-reported by the patient.

Other Eating Disorders

In the *DSM-IV*, a major category of eating disorders was called eating disorders not otherwise specified. This catchall diagnosis included those who did not properly meet the criteria for a specific disorder. It was the most common eating disorder diagnosis.

In the *DSM-5*, this classification was changed to other specified feeding or eating disorder (OSFED) or unspecified feeding or eating disorder (UFED). Someone diagnosed with OSFED might have many features of anorexia except the extreme weight loss. They may not meet the threshold of time required for a bulimia or BED diagnosis because they have engaged in bingeing or purging behaviors for less than three months or less frequently than weekly. Others may purge without bingeing. Similarly, a person diagnosed with UFED meets some criteria of an eating disorder (or other *DSM* feeding disorder category) but not all.

These two classifications are important since many people with disordered eating behaviors do not necessarily fit into the narrow categories of anorexia, bulimia, and BED, but they still need a way to get professional help. Some mental health professionals believe eating disorders occur on a spectrum and believe diagnosis should reflect that. Until that time, these categories can help more people get treatment they need.

The Eating Attitudes Test lists statements for a responder to consider, such as, "I avoid eating when I am hungry."[17] Then, the responder chooses "always," "usually," "often," "sometimes," "rarely," or "never." Certain responses to certain statements give a score of 0 to 3. When a trained mental health professional evaluates the responder's answers, they will calculate a total number. Higher numbers generally indicate that the person who took the test needs further evaluation for eating disorders.

Those suffering from eating disorders do not always look like they have a problem, especially in Western societies in which thinness, concern about diet, and exercising are admired. A person's culture has a large effect on what they value in themselves and others. This influence can play a large role in the start of an eating disorder.

CHAPTER THREE

CAUSES OF ANOREXIA AND BULIMIA

Sarah Haight—a fashion writer whose work has appeared in *Vogue*, *Teen Vogue*, *Women's Wear Daily*, and *W* magazine—has discussed the causes of her eating disorder:

> Anorexia is one of the most difficult illnesses to trace the origins of: Its roots are tangled, and the delicate unbinding of each contributing factor can be done only once the patient has truly agreed to get help. In my case, the disease was the product of a complicated mélange [combination] of emotional pain, perfectionism, societal pressure, and genetic bad luck. Every anorexic has a narrative of where things started to go awry [wrong].[18]

Haight's assessment sums up the difficulty of eating disorders: There is no single specific cause to find, fix, or stop. A mix of genetic and biological factors, trauma, stress, and cultural expectations is often to blame. In addition, many who suffer from anorexia and bulimia have other mental health issues that can be part of the cause of—or be worsened by—an eating disorder. They must receive treatment for those along with the eating disorder, which can make recovery even harder. Researchers continue to study individuals with anorexia and bulimia to find things sufferers have in common, but the causes are often a complex, individual mix of emotions, environment, and biology.

Born with It?

A number of research studies have provided evidence that eating disorders can run in families. In fact, someone who has a family member with an eating disorder is 7 to 12 times more likely to also develop an eating disorder than someone without a family history of one. Children who are born to parents who have had anorexia at some point are 10 times more likely to develop anorexia themselves than the general population is.

Ira Sacker, a leader in the field of eating disorders, said that when he first began treating patients with eating disorders, he did not pay much attention to the eating patterns of their parents. He was surprised to discover that many parents admitted they, too, had experienced some kind of disordered eating in their past. He now believes eating disorders have a genetic component, meaning there may be some aspect—researchers are unsure exactly what, since there is no specific "eating disorder gene"—that gets passed down from parent to child. Sacker said,

> Having a family history of eating disorder, addictions, and obsessive-compulsive behavior doesn't guarantee that someone will develop an eating disorder. It does suggest, however, that awareness of the possibility needs to be present, just as there needs to be an awareness of a family history of, say, breast cancer or diabetes.[19]

A study at the Medical College of Virginia at Virginia Commonwealth University focused on identical and fraternal twins. Identical twins develop from the same egg, so they have almost the exact same genes. Fraternal twins develop at the same time from two different eggs, so their genes are less similar. The researchers found that pairs of identical twins had a much higher incidence of eating disorders than fraternal twins did, so the scientists concluded that heredity plays a role in eating disorders. They also pointed out that environmental and emotional factors might make twins particularly susceptible.

If twins are constantly compared with each other and judged as being bigger, taller, thinner, or heavier, their body image may become distorted.

Brain chemistry may also play a role in causing someone to develop anorexia or bulimia. Studies on this topic often consider the role of serotonin, a chemical made by nerve cells. Serotonin affects the digestive system and has been found to play a role in hunger and food cravings. Christopher G. Fairburn, who has done extensive research on eating disorders, said,

> Interestingly, dieting has been shown to affect certain chemical transmitters in the brain, particularly serotonin, and this effect is more pronounced

[noticeable] in women than in men. Since sero-tonin is thought to play a role in the normal control of eating as well as in food selection, this finding is intriguing ... Put simply, it seems that an ab-normality in brain serotonin function may put people at risk of developing bulimia nervosa and that dieting in women may exaggerate [increase] this risk.[20]

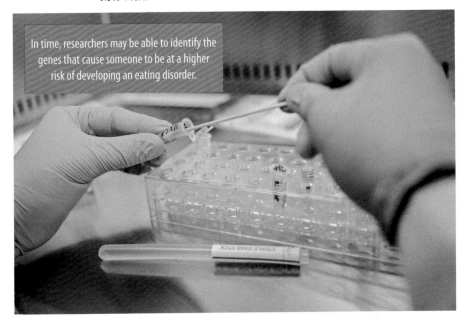

In time, researchers may be able to identify the genes that cause someone to be at a higher risk of developing an eating disorder.

Professor of health education Mark Kittleson pointed out that serotonin is one of the neurotransmitters, or brain chemicals, that give a person a sense of physical and emotional fulfillment. He said, "Serotonin, in particular, sends the message that you feel full and have had enough to eat. Researchers have found that acutely ill patients suffering from anorexia and bulimia have significantly lower levels of serotonin."[21]

Dopamine, a chemical made by the body that takes part in the emotions and pleasure centers of the brain, has also been connected with anorexia and bulimia. Research has found that those with anorexia likely make too much dopamine. Bulimia, on the other hand, is characterized by someone not making enough dopamine, and some experts believe that bingeing may encourage a dopamine release by the brain.

Other Risk Factors

Biology does not determine a person's fate. Although a young man or woman might have a family member with an eating disorder, that does not guarantee that they are also destined to develop one. In fact, one of the greatest risk factors for developing any eating disorder is engaging in diet behavior. The Mayo Clinic states that it is possible that dieting to lose weight may actually cause the brain to change in those who are already at risk. Another risk factor that could push someone with a genetic predisposition toward an eating disorder is stress. The stress could be as simple as moving, starting at a new school, or having a fight with a family member or friend.

However, a stressor could be far more serious and continue to affect a person long after it is over. An event that has occurred that has a strong negative effect on someone is called trauma. Trauma includes any kind of abuse, including physical, emotional, or sexual. It also includes being part of a terrible car accident or natural disaster. Trauma could also occur after witnessing something disturbing, such as a death. According to the Center for Eating Disorders at Sheppard Pratt,

Survivors of trauma often struggle with shame, guilt, body dissatisfaction and a feeling of a lack of control. The eating disorder may become the individual's attempt to regain control or cope with these intense emotions. In some cases, the

eating disorder is an expression of self-harm or misdirected self-punishment for the trauma.[22]

The Negative Effects of Perfectionism

Not all eating disorder patients are overachievers, but many are. One patient with an eating disorder wrote in her journal:

> I cannot recognize or appreciate any of my own accomplishments. Others are always better. Even when I achieve excellence it isn't good enough. I recently got 98 percent on my calculus final and was upset with myself for not doing better. My goals are far too high. I lose sight of what is realistic or even excellent, and strive for what is impossible.[1]

Perfectionists may become procrastinators, putting off important projects because they are afraid they cannot live up to their own high standards, or they may be excessively active. Sacker said,

> Perfectionists will judge their body image by the more unrealistic standards set by the society around us. These demands for perfection are unrealistic and virtually impossible to achieve. They're formed not by the reality of what a healthy body should look like, but by the endless media images of so-called perfect bodies that bombard us every day. That sort of perfection isn't really something any normal person can attain without major body-altering means such as extremely strenuous exercise, starvation dieting, and cosmetic surgery, but the images are still very, very powerful. Combine our societal pressure to be slender with a perfectionist's drive to be perfect, and what you get is someone who will be very vulnerable to a major eating disorder.[2]

1. Quoted in Peggy Claude-Pierre, *The Secret Language of Eating Disorders.* New York, NY: Vintage, 1999, p. 73.

2. Ira Sacker, *Regaining Your Self.* New York, NY: Hyperion, 2007, pp. 58–59.

Comorbidities

Many people who suffer from eating disorders have other mental health issues to deal with. These comorbidities—any two or more disorders that occur at the same time—make treating eating disorders more difficult, but they can also serve as red flags to health care providers that an individual may be at a higher risk of developing an eating disorder.

Often, there is no way to know which mental health issue developed first.

One study found that 97 percent of women being treated at an inpatient hospital for an eating disorder had a comorbidity. Some of these diagnoses, such as depression, anxiety, and abuse of drugs or alcohol, occur across eating disorders and at fairly high rates. Depression is reported as the most common comorbidity among those diagnosed with an eating disorder. Other comorbidities of eating

Common Comorbidities

DEPRESSION	BIPOLAR DISORDER	PANIC AND ANXIETY DISORDERS
loss of interest in previously enjoyed activities, feelings of sadness, loss of energy, feelings of worthlessness	alternating periods of high mood, energy, and activity (manic) and low energy, mood, and activity (depressive)	greater than usual feelings of nervousness or fear about an event, place, or action
POST-TRAUMATIC STRESS DISORDER (PTSD)	OBSESSIVE COMPULSIVE DISORDER (OCD)	OBSESSIVE COMPULSIVE PERSONALITY DISORDER
occurs following a traumatic event; reliving bad memories, feeling anxious or edgy, having trouble sleeping	thoughts that repeat over and over, thoughts or ideas that are not wanted arising, the need to repeat actions many times	obsession with things being neat and orderly, need to feel in control of all situations, inability to make decisions quickly
BORDERLINE PERSONALITY DISORDER	SLEEP DISORDERS	SUBSTANCE ABUSE OR DEPENDENCE
mood swings, problems sustaining personal relationships, feelings of uncertainty about self	problems with getting not enough sleep or too much; problems with getting quality sleep	using drugs or alcohol in a harmful way

These are just a few of the most common comorbidities of people who suffer from eating disorders.

disorders include post-traumatic stress disorder (PTSD), borderline personality disorder, and sleep disorders.

Obsessive-compulsive disorder (OCD) seems to be particularly common among those with anorexia, reinforcing the idea that these sufferers seek perfection, order, and control. The abuse of drugs—especially alcohol—is more likely among those with bulimia.

Society and Expectations

Society often plays a large role in how people feel about themselves. From actors and athletes to the selectively shared world on Instagram, it is easy for people to find others to compare themselves to. Those who are at risk for eating disorders may be even more affected by these outside influences. They provide a body type to aspire to, even if that body type is unrealistic for the average person to achieve. Size 00 models and celebrities are constantly splashed across the media. Heroes and heroines onscreen are generally beautiful and slim. Characters with plump bodies may be supportive best friends, but they are not often the stars.

These characterizations can have serious consequences. Anne Becker, a professor at Harvard Medical School, published a study describing what happened in Fiji, a small island nation in the Pacific Ocean, before and after television arrived. Before American television arrived, Fijians considered the ideal body to be plump, round, and soft. After three years of watching shows such as *Melrose Place* and *Beverly Hills, 90210*, teenage girls showed serious signs of eating disorders. The Harvard study found that Fijian teens who watched three or more nights of TV per week were more likely to consider themselves too fat. They told investigators they had begun dieting and vomiting to control their weight. The study, begun in the mid-1990s, reported that by 2007, 45 percent of girls on the main island of Fiji said they had engaged in purging behaviors.

Although culture affects how people see themselves and others, concern with body image may begin at home with innocent remarks from parents who warn against eating too much and becoming fat. Other relatives might make a comment about someone being chubby or about what or how much they eat. Siblings and classmates are likely to think up even more hurtful nicknames. Some cultures, such as Asian cultures, may be more prone to making these comments than others. Children and teens may begin engaging in disordered eating behavior to uphold the cultural expectations of their family.

Professor of psychology Susan Mendelsohn widens the net of influence even further:

> *Home and school are not the only breeding grounds for body image derailment. What about the candy store clerk who "cuts you off" after a few candy bars, the local hoods who shout insults from their car windows as they pass, or the beloved neighbor who has a nickname for everyone, usually to reflect the opposite of how they appear. The town giant is "Tiny," the city octogenarian [80-year-old] is "Youngun," and you're "Slim," nicknamed with a know-it-all grin.*[23]

Sports Pressure

Successful athletes are under heavy pressure. They set high goals for themselves. They are often more determined and more disciplined than the average individual. The competitive sports environment adds to the pressure. Anxiety about their performances and negative self-judgment can lead to excessive concern about their bodies—and to eating disorders.

Although any athlete can develop an eating disorder, people in activities that emphasize leanness for performance and appearance are at much greater risk. Wrestlers and jockeys who have to meet rigid weight requirements may develop unhealthy ways of losing or gaining weight. Swimming, diving, dancing, track, and gymnastics require strong, light bodies.

In an article written for Vanderbilt University, Ana Cintado explained one reason gymnasts are vulnerable to eating disorders:

> *Anorexia often strikes young women who try to evade [avoid] the natural process of becoming adults and who use excessive measures to maintain a thin and girlish figure—the exact description of what today's female gymnast must accomplish to stay competitive at the highest levels. For these athletes, the onset of womanhood is their biggest fear because it means developing hips or breasts that might hinder their performance. Thus, starving themselves offers the most convenient solution to their problem.*[24]

Many female athletes have found ways to speak out about their struggles with eating disorders. In 2018, Victoria Garrick—a libero on the women's volleyball team at the University of Southern California—talked about her struggle when she joined the high-level sports team as a freshman. She did not want to work out or eat the way she was instructed to for fear her body would change. She said, "Female athletes have pressure from society and Instagram to look one way and then we have pressure from our team and the sports world to look another way. As my body started to get bigger, I could hear my mind start to say 'Don't

eat carbs, don't eat this.'"[25] She found herself turning to food to cope with uncomfortable emotions
regarding her body and the lifestyle pressures of
Division I athletics. Soon, her mental health began
to suffer as well. She ended up taking a break from
playing volleyball to help heal her body and mental
state, but she noted, "It's hard to take time off from
competing for an injury that people can't see."[26]

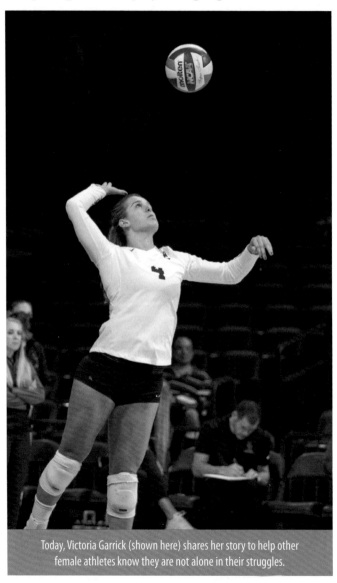

Today, Victoria Garrick (shown here) shares her story to help other
female athletes know they are not alone in their struggles.

Online Communities That Harm

Although much blame has been directed at the fashion and entertainment media for promoting images and behavior that lead to eating disorders, the influence of peer-driven websites may be even more dangerous. Pro-ana (pro-anorexia) and pro-mia (pro-bulimia) websites are created by those suffering from anorexia or bulimia who falsely believe these are legitimate lifestyles rather than serious illnesses. Similar individuals and groups can also be found on social media platforms.

It is easy to find "thinspiration" on websites such as Instagram, Pinterest, and Tumblr. Like pro-ana and pro-mia websites, these platforms can bring together those who want to share tips on being better at their eating disorder and offering motivation to keep going down those paths. For a long time, searching for a hashtag such as #thinspiration was all it took. However, in 2012, Instagram and Tumblr both banned content that promoted any self-harm—including eating disorder behaviors. Many applauded this decision, but as BuzzFeed News pointed out in a 2016 article, the ban may have made the problem worse. Hashtags that were clearly related to thinspiration were no longer allowed on Instagram, but motivated users came up with many variations on these words in order to continue sharing and taking in content they wanted. In fact, a 2015 study by the Georgia Institute of Technology said the ban made engagement with eating disorder hashtags greater on Instagram.

Researchers have offered ways to combat the ever-growing groups of those with eating disorders on platforms such as these, including marking certain posts with a content advisory that contains a link to the NEDA website or redirecting someone who searches for eating disorder content on

Too Much Social Media Pressure

When model and Instagram star Alexis Ren was 17, her mother died of breast cancer. In her grief, she gained a little weight while on location for a modeling job in Australia—a fact that her modeling agency was quick to point out to her. To lose those extra pounds, she began eating less and working out more. She began starring in YouTube videos with a boyfriend who was also a model and worried even more about her appearance. She told *Cosmopolitan* magazine in 2017, "I was my worst critic ever. The only sense of relief I had was to be able to monitor my eating and my workouts."[1]

Ren gained a large following on Instagram during this time—millions of people she felt pressure to maintain a certain image for. However, she was not happy, she did not feel well, and family and friends were beginning to show concern about her exercise and eating habits. Only after breaking up with her boyfriend did she decide to get help.

Today, Ren says she still deals with food guilt

Alexis Ren appeared on *Dancing with the Stars* in 2018.

and that like her grief for her mother, it is always there a little bit. However, she has come a long way, even posting about her struggles on her Instagram.

1. Quoted in Elizabeth Narins, "Instagram Star Alexis Ren Opens Up About the Eating Disorder She Hid For Years," *Cosmopolitan*, May 25, 2017. www.cosmopolitan.com/health-fitness/a9657755/alexis-ren-eating-disorder/.

Tumblr directly to NEDA. However, others say these efforts could further alienate those suffering from eating disorders rather than encourage them to get help.

Is It Catching?

Eating disorders are not contagious in the same way as measles or the flu, but the idea of having an eating disorder can be catching. Seeing websites, groups, or even news stories about someone with anorexia, bulimia, or another eating disorder can lead to someone developing an eating disorder themselves.

The idea of "catching" or "spreading" eating disorders has been around for many years. British psychologist Gerald Russell, who wrote the first paper describing bulimia as a separate illness from anorexia, has even said that he takes "full responsibility" for the disorder's spread by publishing that paper: "There was a common language for it. And knowledge spreads very quickly."[27] Once bulimia nervosa was part of the *DSM*, more papers came out about this "new" eating disorder. The information filtered down into women's magazines such as *Better Homes and Gardens*, which is how such a widespread audience learned about it. According to an article on The Cut, "Psychologists studying the developmental psychopathology of eating disorders have led dozens of controlled experiments finding a near-perfect link between mass media and eating disorder symptoms."[28]

Sometimes an eating disorder such as anorexia is shown to spread throughout a group. At least three members of the British musical group the Spice Girls, who were popular in the late 1990s and early 2000s, have admitted to suffering from eating disorders. Geri Halliwell (Ginger Spice) said she developed eating disorders while living with the other Spice Girls. She felt she was fat compared to other band members and developed bulimia while trying to lose weight. Victoria Beckham (Posh Spice) said that Geri encouraged her and Melanie Chisholm (Sporty Spice) to take up running and to eat liquid meals. Eventually, Beckham started to binge eat; at one point, she ate 10 bowls of cereal in one sitting. Chisholm starved herself and exercised excessively. She admitted in 2017, "I started to restrict my food to a point where I was just … eating fruit and vegetables."[29]

The causes of anorexia and bulimia are complex. Compounded by cultural pressure, societal expectations, risk factors, and comorbidities, it may seem very difficult to treat the mental health aspects of eating disorders—and it is. However, the medical consequences of an eating disorder are also complicated and often must be addressed before any psychiatric work is done.

CHAPTER FOUR

MEDICAL COMPLICATIONS

When Karen Carpenter died in 1983, the world suddenly knew what the word "anorexia" meant. Even scarier, everyone now knew the deadly consequences of eating disorders. Carpenter had been seeking treatment for her years of dieting, laxatives, and medication that sped up her metabolism. For her, it was help sought too late. Her heart and digestive system were already weak. The Los Angeles coroner reported her cause of death as "heartbeat irregularities brought on by chemical imbalances associated with anorexia nervosa."[30]

Death is the worst outcome of anorexia and bulimia. However, on the way to a terrible event such as the cardiac arrest of Karen Carpenter, there are many other troubling physical complications that can affect an eating disorder sufferer. Still, some choose death when faced with the seriousness of their disorder, medical complications, and other mental health issues.

What Is the Harm?

Although research shows that dieting is a serious risk factor for developing an eating disorder, many people likely do not see skipping a meal here or there as a big deal. Similarly, they may take a laxative after a big meal once in a while. However, these behaviors are a slippery slope. They can lead to

As part of the Carpenters, Karen Carpenter sold more than 80 million albums between 1969 and her death in 1983.

avoiding eating altogether or multiple laxative uses in one day. The eating disorder does not have to be incredibly severe for the body to respond. Over time, medical issues and serious physical problems can arise.

A dentist is sometimes the first to notice when someone engages in self-induced vomiting. Vomit contains a lot of acid, and this acid can damage the teeth, leading to tooth decay and sensitive teeth. It can also cause harm to the esophagus and intestines. Those who are purging in this way tend to have an irritated, sore throat that will not go away, and they can develop a long-term problem such as acid reflux. In fact, acid may wear away at the esophagus and stomach so much that either one could rupture.

Those with eating disorders may have many other problems with their digestive system. Both the restriction of calories seen in anorexia as well as vomiting can cause slow digestion and cause constipation. The muscles of the intestines, like all the muscles in the body, need nutrients to function. Without proper nutrition, they can weaken and be unable to properly move food through the digestive tract. Not eating enough may also stop bowel movements because there simply is not enough food in the system to eliminate it. Furthermore, if laxatives are abused, the body may not be able to have a bowel movement without them.

Purging as well as excessive laxative use can cause dehydration or an electrolyte imbalance, which means there is too much or too little sodium, calcium, potassium, or other minerals in the body. Potassium, for example, helps the heart beat and the muscles work correctly. If there is too little of it in the body, someone might experience irregular heartbeats, eventually leading to heart failure. Electrolyte imbalances and dehydration affect the brain. They can lead to seizures or even strokes. The brain also suffers from lack of nutrition. It needs sources of healthy fats to keep the layer of fat around neurons (nerve cells) healthy and strong. Without it, this layer can be damaged, and the person's hands, feet, and limbs may tingle or go numb.

Fats also contribute to the creation of hormones throughout the body. Those who are not eating enough fat or calories can cause their hormone levels to fall, causing irregularity of menstruation or amenorrhea in women.

Taking in too few calories causes other body tissues to break down, too. Since the body needs fuel, it starts to break itself down to use for energy. This often starts with muscle—and because the heart is primarily made of muscle, this breakdown can be particularly problematic. It can cause blood pressure and heart rate to drop as the heart cannot pump the way it needs to.

An eating disorder such as anorexia or bulimia can affect the body down to the cellular level. The body's metabolic rate falls with a lack of food to burn and use for energy. This often makes eating disorder sufferers cold and can even cause them to develop hypothermia, which is when the internal body temperature drops too low. They may stop making enough of some kinds of blood cells. Anemia occurs when someone does not have enough red blood cells or is not taking in enough iron. It makes a person feel tired, weak, and short of breath. Poor nutrition also decreases the number of white blood cells in the blood, meaning there are fewer to fight disease and infection.

Looking Long-Term

There are long-term health issues that can come about from anorexia and bulimia. Low levels of certain sex hormones can cause osteopenia and osteoporosis, which are a weakening and loss of bone in the body. Once bone loss has begun, it cannot be reversed, only managed. The risk of broken bones remains higher for people who have these conditions for the rest of their lives. Additionally, irregularities in the menstrual cycle can cause a woman to have trouble getting pregnant. Women who have suffered from anorexia have higher miscarriage rates and lower rates of carrying a baby to term. Women with bulimia are at risk of a relapse when they do get pregnant.

People who binge as part of their eating disorder often do so on foods that are considered very tasty, such as those high in sugar, fat, and salt. Even if these foods are purged by vomiting or using laxatives, parts of them can remain in the body to be digested. Over time, intake of these foods can disrupt how the body deals with the hormone insulin, which regulates blood sugar. Type II diabetes is a possible result of a prolonged diet of these kinds of foods.

It is also important to remember that the physical issues that are caused by eating disorders only get worse the longer someone restricts, purges, or otherwise engages in eating disorder behaviors. Given enough time, many of these issues—particularly those having to do with the brain and heart—can cause death.

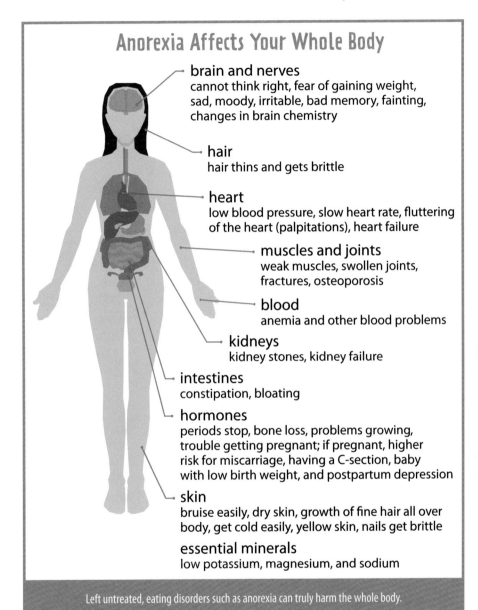

Anorexia Affects Your Whole Body

brain and nerves
cannot think right, fear of gaining weight, sad, moody, irritable, bad memory, fainting, changes in brain chemistry

hair
hair thins and gets brittle

heart
low blood pressure, slow heart rate, fluttering of the heart (palpitations), heart failure

muscles and joints
weak muscles, swollen joints, fractures, osteoporosis

blood
anemia and other blood problems

kidneys
kidney stones, kidney failure

intestines
constipation, bloating

hormones
periods stop, bone loss, problems growing, trouble getting pregnant; if pregnant, higher risk for miscarriage, having a C-section, baby with low birth weight, and postpartum depression

skin
bruise easily, dry skin, growth of fine hair all over body, get cold easily, yellow skin, nails get brittle

essential minerals
low potassium, magnesium, and sodium

Left untreated, eating disorders such as anorexia can truly harm the whole body.

Mortality

Anorexia has the highest mortality, or death, rate of all psychiatric disorders. One study published in 2016 found that, when compared with peers who did not have eating disorders, those with anorexia were five times more likely to die by the time the study was completed. Another study found that someone with anorexia who has binged and purged in the past was more likely to have died. Some researchers have reported that bulimia seems to have a lower mortality rate that anorexia, but it still has serious health consequences.

Death rates for eating disorders for the general population are hard to know for sure for a few reasons. The percentage of those who died often depends on the severity of the eating disorders in the population studied. Some studies do not have enough participants to give rates that can be generalized well. Other researchers look at many studies and form a conclusion based on these without collecting new data. Most of all, sometimes eating disorders are not reported as the cause of a death. Instead, another health problem will be reported as the cause, even if that problem was caused by an eating disorder. For example, if anorexia weakened someone's heart, the cause of death might be listed as heart failure.

About 30 to 40 percent of eating disorder sufferers engage in self-harm of some kind. This increases their likelihood of death through accidental injury. These behaviors can also escalate into thoughts of suicide.

Compared to the general population, people with eating disorders such as anorexia and bulimia are much more likely to commit suicide. Studies have shown that around 17 percent of people diagnosed with anorexia attempt suicide. In fact, about one in every five deaths attributed to anorexia is a suicide. Michael Rollin, a psychiatrist at the Eating Disorder Center of Denver, gave *Social Work Today* some insight as to why the suicide rate is so high:

> *It [anorexia] not only takes over their behavior*
> *but their physical health and the content of their*

minds. One of the biggest frustrations of people with eating disorders is that it's what they spend their day thinking about, planning around, and essentially doing all day long. It hijacks their lives and in that way, they often feel like they have no respite [relief].[31]

Researchers in one small study found that in these cases, the sufferer showed a genuine wish to die. The suicides studied were carried out in ways that would be difficult to prevent and did not have

Christy Henrich: Dying for a Medal

Christy Henrich was a world-class American gymnast. She made the U.S. national gymnastics team, and in 1988, placed ninth at the Olympic Trials. In 1989, she won the silver medal in the all-around U.S. National Championships. She represented the United States at the World Championships in Stuttgart, Germany, placing fourth with the American team. One balance beam leap that she originated was named after her, and it is still included in the Code of Points for artistic gymnastics.

When a judge at the international meet in Stuttgart told Christy she needed to lose weight, she took the comment to heart, and a five-year battle with her body began. She developed full-blown anorexia; her 4-foot 11-inch (150 cm) frame shrank to less than 60 pounds (27.2 kg). Her alarmed family forced her to enter a hospital. She went through periods of recovery, relapses, and numerous treatments, but it was too late: The damage done to her body was too severe. Eight days after her 22nd birthday, Christy died of multiple organ failure.

Her death caused a spotlight to be turned on the problem of eating disorders in gymnasts. Kim Arnold, a U.S. team member in the 1990s, said, "There was a lot of eating and purging. You used to see how little you can eat today and still get through a workout. We used to see how many meals we could miss before we had to eat again."[1]

According to Ron Thompson, an eating disorder specialist who has consulted with the Indiana University athletic department, the gymnasts' youth and their driven personalities plus the competitive environment puts them at high risk for eating disorders. "These kids are so mentally tough, so willing to do anything the coach says will make them a better athlete," Thompson said. "They're perfectionists so continuing to train on broken bones and having eating disorders is normal behavior to them."[2]

1. Quoted in Scott M. Reid, "Emphasis on Thin Is a Heavy Burden," *GYM Media Report*, January 16, 2005. www.gymmedia.com/FORUM/agforum/05_01_henrich_e.htm.

2. Quoted in Reid, "Emphasis on Thin Is a Heavy Burden."

anything to do with starvation, restricting food, or other characteristic eating disorder behaviors. A licensed clinical social worker at the Renfrew Center of New York, Connie Quinn, said this would make sense: "The self-loathing associated with anorexia is so punishing that it wouldn't seem extraordinary to me that extreme measures might be taken to end that suffering."[32]

Getting Help

Someone suffering from bulimia or anorexia may not be able to see beyond their eating disorder to understand the great danger they are in. A friend, family member, teacher, or doctor might be the person to bring up health issues they see, whether physical or mental. For some, that might be enough to seek help on their own. They might opt for outpatient treatment, which means living at home but seeing a therapist, dietician, and other health professionals to begin working through their disordered behaviors. However, many sufferers may feel angry or deny they have a problem. They may not willingly participate in outpatient services for their eating disorder. In some cases, they may need to be checked into an inpatient hospital specializing in eating disorders. This process generally starts when someone with anorexia or bulimia has a serious medical issue and they are checked into a hospital to deal with it. Very low blood pressure, electrolyte imbalances, and low core body temperature are all reasons for someone with an eating disorder to be seen in a hospital. Once they are medically stable, they will go through a physical and psychiatric evaluation to see if their case is serious enough for an inpatient hospital. A decline in weight despite trying other outpatient interventions for the eating disorder or a weight that is less than about

Kesha

Music artist Kesha told *Rolling Stone* in 2017 that she always felt like an outsider in the entertainment industry. She remembers eating lunch in the bathroom in middle school and compared her feeling of being an outcast today to that feeling. In addition, she felt pressure to look a certain way in order to keep her career in music going.

However, the shame she began to feel when she ate took a toll on her. She would make herself throw up to undo any meals she did eat. The weight loss that stemmed from this behavior got her positive attention—which she found confusing. She said, "I was slowly, slowly starving myself. And the worse I got and the sicker I got, the better a lot of people around me were saying that I looked. They would just be like, 'Oh, my gosh, keep doing whatever you're doing! You look so beautiful, so stunning.'"[1]

Eventually, Kesha was tired of hiding the food she did not eat at dinner parties and no longer wanted to keep so many secrets. She turned to her mother, with whom she was very close. Her mom sent her to a rehabilitation center to recover, where she met with someone to help her with nutrition and relearned how to eat healthily. Over time, she realized how powerful the experience was. She chose to live a full life instead of one filled with shame and self-hate.

Kesha's 2017 album *Rainbow* was a product of her healing and recovery. Critics described the album as showing Kesha's hope, love, and belief in herself.

1. Quoted in Brian Hiatt, "The Liberation of Kesha," *Rolling Stone*, October 4. 2017. www.rollingstone.com/music/music-features/the-liberation-of-kesha-123984/.

75 percent of a healthy weight are two reasons inpatient hospitals might be considered. Additionally, having suicidal thoughts or depression or being unable to take care of oneself also may cause someone to be placed in an inpatient hospital.

When someone is admitted to an inpatient hospital specializing in eating disorders, their immediate needs are met first. This may include further medical intervention to keep them alive and medically stable. In a hospital specializing in eating disorders, a person has many health professionals to help, day and night. These include a medical doctor who will treat the physical complications of their eating disorder. Patients will also see a therapist who specializes in eating disorders to begin the difficult work of stabilizing their mental health. They will also begin to work with a dietician or other nutrition professional to start monitoring how much and what the patient eats. If the patient refuses to eat enough—or at all—a tube may be inserted into their nose and down their throat to feed them directly. This intensive refeeding is sometimes also necessary for eating disorder sufferers who are too weak to feed themselves yet.

For many, a stay at an inpatient hospital is an important step toward treatment and recovery. However, it is very expensive to stay in one of these facilities, so most people do not stay very long. When they are released, most continue with outpatient treatment. Treatment for anorexia and bulimia is multifaceted, and although the road to recovery is long, it is possible to reach the destination of health—both mental and physical.

CHAPTER FIVE

TREATMENT AND RECOVERY

Treating anorexia and bulimia is much like working on a very difficult puzzle. First, doctors need to put the pieces together for a diagnosis. Next, the underlying causes of the eating disorder need to be explored. Does this patient have anxiety or a family history of eating disorders? Have they endured some kind of trauma? Finally, family, friends, and medical professionals must convince a patient with anorexia or bulimia that they need help. Some people who have eating disorders refuse to believe their behavior can have serious effects and do not seek help until it is too late to save their lives. Others feel their lives are worthless and that they do not deserve help. Only when the person with the eating disorder is willing to participate can a treatment plan begin to take shape.

The final picture of eating disorder diagnosis and treatment looks different for every patient, which is another reason that these disorders are hard to treat. There is no one-size-fits-all approach. While one person may do well in group therapy alone, another may need medication and nutrition help. Few people are able to fully recover on their own. The process of recovering from an eating disorder is challenging—and it may last for the rest of a person's life.

Treatment Goals

The very first goal of any treatment of an eating

disorder, including anorexia and bulimia, is restoring the patient's health. For those who are hospitalized, immediate health issues, such as very low blood pressure, are handled first. All those with eating disorders, whether their treatment starts in a hospital or not, are evaluated for health issues that need to be treated right away. Then, their team of medical professionals begins to work toward bettering their nutritional status. For example, someone with anorexia who has been eating very few calories will slowly increase calorie intake. For many, this will include adding in supplements such as vitamins to make sure the body is getting the micronutrients it has not been getting.

Over time, eating more helps sufferers reach a healthy weight. However, adding in more food can be difficult physically and should be closely monitored. Those in treatment may experience bloating or constipation. This step can be difficult psychologically as well. Feelings of anxiety, frustration, and stress about eating are likely to come up. That is why another treatment goal is to work toward a healthy relationship with eating, food, and the body. Many organizations and noted eating disorder specialists believe that both the physical and emotional problems underlying anorexia and bulimia have to be treated, but exploring the psychological problems that led to the development of the disorder can only begin once serious medical problems have been treated and weight restoration has begun.

Many factors have to be considered when working out the type of treatment that will be most likely to succeed with a particular patient. These include the person's age, their overall physical condition, how quickly the patient has been losing weight, the length of their illness, and information about previous treatments. Also important is how willing the patient is to cooperate in exploring the psychological problems underlying the disease.

Firsthand Experience

Many therapists who are now working in the field of eating disorders have been victims of these diseases themselves. Lindsey Hall recovered from bulimia and went on to write several books on eating disorders with her husband, Leigh Cohn. Hall was the first person who recovered from bulimia to appear on national television. Both she and her husband have lectured extensively on eating disorders and served as officers of nonprofit eating disorder associations. They are well-known authorities worldwide in the field of eating disorders. Their books have been translated into Japanese, Chinese, Italian, and other languages. Hall's understanding of eating disorders has been acquired through long years of close association with these disorders. She wrote,

> In a perfect world, free from eating disorders, all people would appreciate that love and self-esteem are their birthright regardless of shape or weight. Families, aware of the causes and consequences of eating disorders, would be a constant source of communication and sharing ... Food would be a symbol of life rather than a tool for abuse. In other words, people would be allowed to be themselves without conforming to tight-fitting roles based on artificial limits.[1]

1. Lindsey Hall and Leigh Cohn, *Bulimia: A Guide to Recovery.* Carlsbad, CA: Gürze, 1999, p. 73.

Therapy

When an eating disorder has been going on for some time, professional help is generally necessary to repair the psychological damage it has done and to stop it from getting worse. Psychotherapy is a form of treatment that involves discussions between a therapist and a single patient or a group of patients. It is also known as talk therapy, counseling, or psychosocial therapy. Individual psychological treatment is most common for adults, especially those who live alone. Many types of individual therapy are available. A type of talk therapy called cognitive behavioral therapy (CBT) helps the patient identify unhealthy, negative beliefs and behaviors and replace them with healthy, positive ones. It is based on the idea that a person's thoughts, not other people or situations, determine how a person behaves. CBT has proven to be especially beneficial in treating bulimia. It is also used to treat anorexia.

A newer type of therapy called dissonance-based (DB) has shown good results in treating eating disorders. In this type of therapy, people examine the messages society is sending them about their bodies—especially the need to be thin in order to be beautiful and worthy of love—and learn how to identify the problems with those messages. The idea is that once people understand more about the negative messages they are being sent, they will be better able to resist them. DB sessions can take place either one-on-one with a therapist or in a group setting.

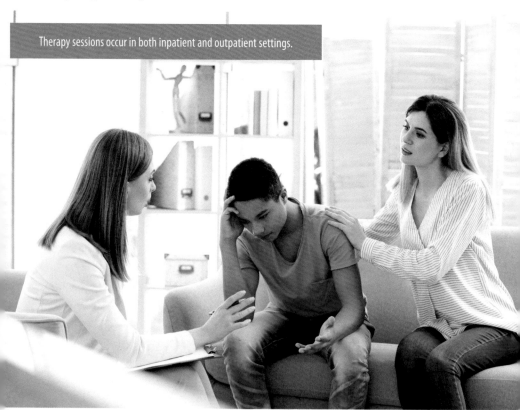

Therapy sessions occur in both inpatient and outpatient settings.

Interpersonal therapy focuses on the person's current relationships with other people. The goal of this therapy is to improve the person's skills in relating to others, including family, friends, and coworkers. The patient learns how to evaluate the way they interact with others and develop strategies for dealing with relationships and communication problems.

Family therapy is especially important for children or young adults who still live at home. It can help concerned family members learn the best ways to help the patient. It can also resolve family conflicts and uncover family problems that may have been at the root of the eating disorder. Author Steven Levenkron said family therapy can be a powerful tool for bringing about rapid change in the relationships that contribute to eating disorders: "[Family therapy] is a setting where often the 'unsayable' (at home) can now be said because a 'referee' is present; a setting where a family can use the therapist as a teacher and role model who can step back, analyze the conflict, and resolve it."[33]

A form of family therapy developed by researchers at the Maudsley Hospital in London, England, has received worldwide attention. It focuses on patients who are acutely ill with anorexia. In this method, the family is seen as the most important resource at the therapist's disposal. The family is not blamed for the illness. Instead, the Maudsley therapist tries to empower the family to assume the responsibility for nurturing their ill child back to health. Despite the fact that this may be frightening to the family, the therapist encourages them with warm acceptance and gives them the expertise to change their child's destructive behavior.

Group psychotherapy is often used together with individual psychotherapy in both inpatient and

Animal Companions

Some therapists are turning to innovative kinds of treatment. David Herzog, an internationally renowned expert on eating disorders, recommends using pets in treating patients. Touch and trust, he says, are very important in the healing process.

Caroline Knapp, one of his patients, has written a memoir, *Pack of Two: The Intricate Bond Between People and Dogs*. In this book, Knapp relates her experience with anorexia and the way in which her pets help her stay well. She wrote, "Put a leash in my hand, put Lucille [her dog] by my side, and something happens, something magical, something clicks inside, as though some key piece of me, missing for years, has suddenly slid into place, and I know I'll be okay."[1]

The use of horses in residential programs is growing in popularity. Remuda Ranch in Arizona was one of the first to use equine therapy in treating eating disorders. Each patient rides two or three times a week on a particular horse that is assigned to them. Sharon Simpson, director of Remuda Ranch, said the bond that develops between horse and rider creates a sense of unconditional acceptance that many patients have never experienced before. "Perfection," said Simpson, "does not enter the relationship. The horse is a living breathing animal, and because of that, he can be unpredictable, just like life is unpredictable."[2]

Therapy animals are specially trained to be friendly and calm in places such as hospitals.

1. Quoted in Aimee Liu, *Gaining*. New York, NY: Grand Central, 2008, p. 132.

2. Quoted in Liu, *Gaining*, p. 134.

outpatient settings. Different groups have different goals. Some groups focus on food, eating, body image, interpersonal skills, and job training. Other groups focus on understanding the psychological factors that may have led to the development of the disorder. The participants learn that they are not alone in their struggles. Their interactions (under the guidance of a therapist) include both supporting and confronting each other.

Sharing experiences in a group can be effective in reducing guilt, shame, and feelings of isolation. Group discussions can also lead to insights about strategies for recovery. There are potential downsides to group therapy; for instance, the youngest members may learn new ways to lose weight or, as sometimes happens in a group of people with anorexia, some may compete to be the thinnest person. However, on the whole, most experts agree that group therapy is generally more beneficial than harmful in treating eating disorders.

Taking Medication

When psychotherapy is not enough to help a patient with anorexia or bulimia, medications may be prescribed. According to the NIMH, antidepressants, antipsychotics, and mood-stabilizing medications can be helpful in treating eating disorders and their comorbidities, such as depression and anxiety. Someone suffering from an eating disorder who also experiences another mental health condition will work closely with their medical team to determine the right dosage of medication—a process that can take patience and time.

Antidepressants are used in cases of bulimia to help treat disordered eating behaviors, depression, and anxiety while a patient is also undergoing therapy. According to the Cleveland Clinic, medication can help someone reduce their binges. The most commonly prescribed type of antidepressant is a selective serotonin reuptake inhibitor (SSRI), which stops the brain from reabsorbing too much serotonin after it is initially released. The U.S. Food and Drug Administration (FDA) has approved Prozac (fluoxetine) to treat bulimia, but other medications in its class of SSRIs have also been shown to be helpful. SSRIs seem to be less successful in treating anorexia, but another kind of

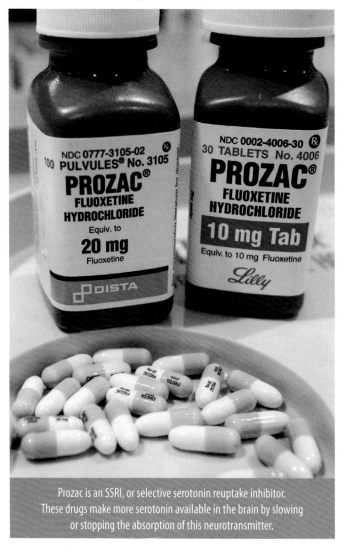

Prozac is an SSRI, or selective serotonin reuptake inhibitor. These drugs make more serotonin available in the brain by slowing or stopping the absorption of this neurotransmitter.

antidepressant called a tricyclic antidepressant may be more helpful in this area. Tricyclics increase the level of neurotransmitters such as serotonin in the brain. Research has shown that low levels of serotonin may be responsible for depression and also for the urge to binge or purge.

Anxiety may be one of the contributing causes of eating disorders, and it is likely to increase as the patient worries about undergoing treatment for the disease. Antianxiety drugs can be prescribed to help patients feel calmer. However, the body develops a tolerance to them, so they become less effective over time.

As happens with many effective but powerful drugs, medications used to help patients with anorexia and bulimia can have troublesome side effects. These may include tiredness, confusion, and low blood pressure. Therefore, it is important that patients taking them have ongoing medical supervision. Experts agree that medication alone is rarely a solution to recovery from an eating disorder. However, when combined with psychotherapy, medication can be helpful.

Support Groups

Support groups can be life-saving when their goal is to help members overcome their eating disorders and maintain healthy lifestyles. On the other hand, support groups that encourage members to think of their diseases as lifestyles can be deadly. In these groups, members learn ways to support their illnesses and share tricks to hide them from others. With a little research, reliable support groups can be found, and most of them are free. Some support groups focus on behaviors that are related to eating disorders. Others deal with underlying emotional issues as well as behaviors.

Going to a support group for the first time can be a scary experience—especially for a person who has been hiding their disease. Jennie, who suffered from bulimia, described her first experience of attending a support group recommended by her doctor: "I didn't think I was going to be able to walk through the door. My whole body was shaking … Even though the atmosphere was casual, it was hard to open up at first."[34] Although her story was different from the others' in the group, as she listened to them talk, she realized they had things in common. "If they were going to make an effort to get over this," Jennie said, "I had no excuse not to try as well."[35]

Not every support group is the right fit for every person. It may take someone time to find a group they feel comfortable sharing in, but it is worth it.

Recovery

When victims of anorexia and bulimia accept the fact that their diseases are controlling their lives and become willing to make necessary changes, they can hope to overcome them. Experts agree that no one with severe bulimia or anorexia finds healing to be a neat, orderly, or predictable process. Slipping back into old hurtful habits of behavior during treatment and relapses after treatment ends are common. Commenting on celebrities who have been "cured" of an eating disorder, Ira Sacker said, "Actors and models appearing on talk shows make it sound as if getting over an eating disorder is quick and easy, but the reality is very different. Every step of the way is paved with speed bumps, and progress is slow and uneven, with plenty of setbacks."[36]

Michael Strober, director of the Eating Disorder Program at the University of California, Los Angeles, (UCLA) Neuropsychiatric Institute, has treated eating disorders for more than 30 years. At UCLA, he said, patients with anorexia and bulimia are considered recovered "when they maintain a healthy weight and no longer obsessively count calories, binge or purge or manically exercise."[37] For women, regaining their menstrual cycle is a key sign that they are recovering too.

However, even years later, these recovered patients show abnormally high rates of anxiety and obsessive thinking, especially perfectionism. "The solution," Strober said, "is not to eliminate these traits but to learn to manage them. So in treatment we try to move patients to a new framework, to enable them to accept growth and change."[38]

It is also vitally important for them to learn to recognize and avoid triggers that may cause a recurrence of their symptoms. Finding ways to prevent these diseases is the best hope for reducing the number of victims. Fortunately, many organizations and specialists are involved in this process.

Relapse

Despite stories of celebrities who go to rehab centers for a few weeks and emerge cured of their eating disorders, the road to recovery is seldom short or straight. The website Anorexia Nervosa & Related Eating Disorders (ANRED) estimated that about 60 percent of people who have eating disorders fully recover. Of the remaining 40 percent, about half will partially recover and half will deal with their eating disorder for life.

Recovery involves not only physical progress but also emotional healing. After many years of treating patients with eating disorders, Sacker put the stumbling blocks for patients into four categories: slips, lapses, relapses, and collapses.

Slips are irrational thoughts that originate in the patient's mind. A patient with anorexia might have negative thoughts about eating. A patient with bulimia might think about what they have eaten and about ways to purge it from their body. If the patient hides these kinds of irrational, negative thoughts from their therapist, the thoughts may build up until they lead to a lapse.

A lapse occurs when the patient acts out their irrational thinking. It is generally limited and brief—for example, skipping only one meal—but it is scary for the patients and may make them feel as if they are failures. The therapist will try to make the patient understand that lapses are common and are to be expected on the way to recovery.

A relapse is far more serious. It is a return to the eating behavior that made the patient sick. "The difference between a lapse and relapse," Sacker said, "is the difference between a stumble and a bad fall. When you stumble, you can catch yourself in the midst of it; when you fall, you can't stop yourself at all."[39]

With proper treatment, the relapse may be turned around. However, if it is not caught and stopped immediately, it may become a collapse—a full-blown return of the original eating disorder behavior. In fact, it may become an even more intense form of the disorder or even another type of eating disorder. Patients sometimes go through more than one cycle of relapse and collapse. They may require medical attention to repair physical damage to their bodies or psychiatric care and medication to prevent suicide.

Living in Recovery

Many people who have suffered from acute eating disorders are now happy, productive individuals. They may have had lapses and relapses on the way to recovery. Eventually, however, they have learned ways to cope with the obsessive feelings that still return from time to time. This is especially necessary in times of stress.

Nicole, who survived bulimia, said her recovery was neither easy nor completely secure. However, during treatment, she learned strategies for overcoming the impulses that might trigger a relapse. "There are times even now," she said, "five years later—that I find myself in a food panic. But now, whenever I feel the urge to chow and purge an entire cake, I stop myself and ask, 'Why? Am I really hungry? Or is it because I'm anxious or feeling pressured by something else?'"[40] Each time she makes it safely through the panic attack, her self-confidence grows. She said, "Now I know I'm in charge. Every time I beat that feeling, it's like saying, 'This is my body and my life.'"[41]

Joyce Maynard is a writer who became obsessed with her weight and body shape in her late teens. She trained herself to monitor every bite of food that entered her mouth. If she let herself slip and eat a piece of bread or a piece of chocolate, she felt self-hatred and disgust. She convinced herself that food was her enemy.

Then, she entered into a relationship with a man who tried to tell her what to eat and how much to eat. She rebelled and started to sneak food. She would binge and then vomit to get rid of the calories. She no longer knew how to eat like a normal person. "I knew only two conditions," she said, "total denial, total indulgence."[42] After becoming a mother, she gradually and painfully learned to eat normally.

Thirty years later, the wiring in her brain caused by her disordered eating is still there. She compared herself to an alcoholic who has been sober for 30 years and still speaks of herself as "recovering." She said, "All these years later, in bed at night, I sometimes still run my hand over my ribs, to make sure I can still feel them. I can tell you the exact number of calories in a cashew."[43] When she imagines herself getting the flu and throwing up for a couple of days, she hears an internal voice, as if from a radio station, whispering in her ear, "'Oh good, I bet I'll drop four pounds.' I no longer expect," Maynard continued, "this voice will ever be silenced entirely. All I can do is take it in, and change the station."[44]

Prevention

It is nearly impossible to know who will develop anorexia or bulimia. Medical professionals can identify those who are at high risk for developing them, but even that can be hard to know without a detailed family history, honest conversations about dieting, and careful monitoring of a person's body weight. This means that prevention of eating disorders in all populations should be the goal.

Overcoming an eating disorder takes a lot of work. However, enjoying food is part of life, and everyone should have the chance to eat without a care in the world.

The Mayo Clinic suggests ways for parents to prevent eating disorders in their children, but they can be applied to everyone. First, the organization advises avoiding dieting. Instead, people should learn to enjoy food and understand how a balanced diet helps their health, both physical and mental. Next, if a person sees portrayals of bodies on TV or online that trouble them or cause disturbing thoughts, it is important for them to talk to a trusted friend or adult. Finally, everyone should work to maintain a healthy body image. This can be difficult if a person's friends participate in body shaming of themselves or others. Young adults can be the voice of reason who reminds everyone that body shapes vary. They can also avoid criticizing their own body, instead replacing negative thoughts with positive ones, such as "My legs are strong and

I am a fast runner." This practice will improve their own body image as well as their peers'. There are many organizations that work to spread this message, and anyone can become part of one of them. By helping to change the culture around them, they are helping to prevent eating disorders.

Finally, the first line of defense against eating disorders is friends and family. If someone notices any warning signs of anorexia, bulimia, or any other eating disorder, they should say something. It may be easier for them to enlist the help of a guidance counselor, coach, or parent. A loved one's concern could be the reason someone gets the help they need before their disorder goes too far.

Anorexia and bulimia are complex mental disorders that millions of people around the world suffer from. However, each of these individuals feels alone in their disorder. By doing further research to help understand anorexia and bulimia, medical professionals and—more importantly—the family and friends of these sufferers can better make these individuals feel seen, heard, and helped.

Chapter One:
Eating Disorders Explained

1. "What Are Eating Disorders?," NEDA, accessed on September 28, 2018. www.nationaleatingdisorders.org/what-are-eating-disorders.

2. Liliana Dell'Osso, et al., "Historical Evolution of the Concept of Anorexia Nervosa and Relationships with Orthorexia Nervosa, Autism, and Obsessive-Compulsive Spectrum," National Institutes of Health, July 7, 2016. www.ncbi.nlm.nih.gov/pmc/articles/PMC4939998/.

3. "What Are Eating Disorders?," NEDA.

4. Quoted in Nick Wilson, "An Eating Disorder Nearly Derailed His MLB Dream. Now This Former Catcher Is Raising Awareness," *The Tribune*, August 8, 2018. www.sanluisobispo.com/news/health-and-medicine/article216205995.html.

Chapter Two:
Warning Signs

5. "Eating Disorders," National Institute of Mental Health, accessed on September 28, 2018. www.nimh.nih.gov/health/topics/eating-disorders/index.shtml.

6. Quoted in Mark J. Kittleson, ed., *The Truth About Eating Disorders*. New York, NY: Facts On File, 2005, p. 70.

7. Mayo Clinic Staff, "Eating Disorders," Mayo Clinic, February 22, 2108. www.mayoclinic.org/diseases-conditions/eating-disorders/symptoms-causes/syc-20353603.

8. Quoted in Gabrielle Olya, "Candace Cameron Bure on Her Struggles with Bulimia: 'It Was Never About the Weight, It Was an Emotional Issue,'" *People*, May 4, 2016. people.com/bodies/candace-cameron-bure-opens-up-about-her-struggles-with-an-eating-disorder/.

9. "Bulimia Nervosa," NEDA, accessed on September 28, 2018. www.nationaleatingdisorders.org/learn/by-eating-disorder/bulimia.

10. "Male Eating Disorder Awareness and Treatment," American Addiction Centers, last updated July 31, 2018. americanaddictioncenters.org/male-eating-disorders/.

11. "Male Eating Disorder Awareness and Treatment," American Addiction Centers.

12. "Male Eating Disorder Awareness and Treatment," American Addiction Centers.

13. Brian C. Harrington, et al., "Initial Evaluation, Diagnosis, and Treatment of Anorexia Nervosa and Bulimia Nervosa," *American Family Physician*, January 1, 2015. www.aafp.org/afp/2015/0101/p46.html.

14. Harrington, et al., "Initial Evaluation, Diagnosis, and Treatment of Anorexia Nervosa and Bulimia Nervosa."

15. Harrington, et al., "Initial Evaluation, Diagnosis, and Treatment of Anorexia Nervosa and Bulimia Nervosa."

16. Harrington, et al., "Initial Evaluation, Diagnosis, and Treatment of Anorexia Nervosa and Bulimia Nervosa."

17. Psych Central Researchers, "Eating Attitudes Test," Psych Cental, last updated July 25, 2018. psychcentral.com/quizzes/eating-attitudes-test/.

Chapter Three:
Causes of Anorexia and Bulimia

18. Quoted in Kate Taylor, ed., *Going Hungry.* New York, NY: Anchor, 2008, pp. 181–182.

19. Ira Sacker, *Regaining Your Self.* New York, NY: Hyperion, 2007, p. 162.

20. Christopher G. Fairburn, *Overcoming Binge Eating.* New York, NY: Guilford, 1995, p. 74.

21. Kittleson, ed., *The Truth About Eating Disorders*, p. 45.

22. "What Causes An Eating Disorder?," The Center for Eating Disorders at Sheppard Pratt, accessed on October 1, 2018. eatingdisorder.org/eating-disorder-information/underlying-causes/.

23. Susan Mendelsohn, *It's Not About the Weight.* Lincoln, NE: iUniverse, 2007, p. 14.

24. Ana Cintado, "Eating Disorders and Gymnastics," Vanderbilt University Psychology Department. healthpsych.psy.vanderbilt.edu/HealthPsych/gymnasts.htm.

25. "USC Volleyball Star Talks Eating Disorders and Mental Health in Female Athletes," YouTube video, 3:57, posted by POPSUGAR, March 27, 2018. www.youtube.com/watch?v=Qqdbzqpc3QM.

26. "USC Volleyball Star Talks Eating Disorders and Mental Heath in Female Athletes," YouTube video, posted by POPSUGAR.

27. Quoted in Lee Daniel Kravetz, "The Strange, Contagious History of Bulimia," The Cut, July 31, 2017. www.thecut.com/article/ how-bulimia-became-a-medical-diagnosis. html.

28. Kravetz, "The Strange, Contagious History of Bulimia."

29. Quoted in Anna Duff, "Mel C Speaks About Battling an Eating Disorder While in the Spice Girls," *Look*, October 4, 2017. www.look.co.uk/ news/mel-c-eating-disorder-595972.

Chapter Four:
Medical Complications

30. Quoted in Fred Bronson, *Billboard's Hottest Hot 100 Hits*, 3rd ed. New York, NY: Billboard Books, 2003, p. 48.

31. Quoted in Lindsey Getz, "Anorexia to Suicide—The Desperate Path," *Social Work Today*, accessed on October 2, 2018. www.socialworktoday.com/news/enews_0812_01.shtml.

32. Quoted in Getz, "Anorexia to Suicide."

Chapter Five:
Treatment and Recovery

33. Steven Levenkron, *Anatomy of Anorexia*. New York, NY: W.W. Norton, 2000, p. 113.

34. Quoted in Kittleson, ed., *The Truth About Eating Disorders*, p. 136.

35. Quoted in Kittelson, ed., *The Truth About Eating Disorders*, p. 136.

36. Sacker, *Regaining Your Self*, p. 167.

37. Quoted in Aimee Liu, *Gaining*. New York, NY: Grand Central, 2008, p. 22.

38. Quoted in Liu, *Gaining*, p. 22.

39. Sacker, *Regaining Your Self*, pp. 129–130.

40. Quoted in Christina Chiu, *Eating Disorder Survivors Tell Their Stories*. New York, NY: Rosen, 1999, p. 50.

41. Quoted in Chiu, *Eating Disorder Survivors*, p. 51.

42. Quoted in Taylor, ed., *Going Hungry*, p. 297.

43. Quoted in Taylor, ed., *Going Hungry*, p. 301.

44. Quoted in Taylor, ed., *Going Hungry*, p. 301.

addiction: Physical, emotional, or psychological dependence on something.

anxiety: A mental illness characterized by irrational feelings of fear, worry, and unease.

body mass index (BMI): A calculation using a person's height and weight to assess levels of body fat.

calorie: A measure of energy intake and output in the body.

depression: A mental illness characterized by feelings of hopelessness and sadness or numbness.

diabetes: A disease in which the body cannot control the amount of sugar in the blood because it does not have enough insulin.

diuretics: Chemicals used to increase urination and get rid of excess fluid.

hormone: A substance produced by the body that influences the way the body grows and develops.

hypothermia: A condition in which the temperature of the body gets very low.

hysteria: A state in which one's emotions get so strong they are uncontrollable.

laxative: A medicine that makes it easier for solid waste to pass through the body.

metabolism: The building-up and breaking-down processes of the body.

mineral: A substance that occurs naturally, is found in some foods, and is needed for good health.

neurotransmitter: A substance that carries a signal from one nerve cell in the body to another.

nutrients: Substances that provide nourishment for the body.

obese: Overweight in a way that is unhealthy.

proteins: Molecules made of amino acids that the body needs to function.

self-esteem: Self-respect; confidence in oneself.

serotonin: A chemical in the brain thought to be involved in depression and in the control of food intake.

theory: An idea that is intended to explain facts or events.

therapy: Treatment or counseling aimed at curing physical or psychological problems.

Eating Disorders Foundation of Canada
Suite 230A, 100 Collip Circle Research Park
Western University
London, Ontario
(519) 858-5111
info@edfc.ca
edfc.ca
This nonprofit organization works to raise money for eating disorder research and advocacy. It works in communities across Canada to offer continuing education for eating disorder professionals and aid those who may not have access to proper eating disorder care.

The Emily Program Foundation
5354 Parkdale Drive
Saint Louis Park, MN 55416
(651) 379-6123
emilyprogramfoundation.org
This foundation is dedicated to working to end eating disorders. It tries to spread hope for those who struggle and also advocate for changes that can prevent these disorders and support eating disorder recovery.

Families Empowered and Supporting Treatment of Eating Disorders (F.E.A.S.T.)
P.O. Box 1281
Warrenton, VA 20188
info@feast-ed.org
(855) 503-3278
feast-ed.org
F.E.A.S.T. works internationally to support those who take care of or love someone with an eating disorder. The organization gives information about these disorders and treatment. Additionally, it advocates for more research on these topics to help those with eating disorders in the future. F.E.A.S.T. brings families into the recovery process and gives them a place to turn for help.

**National Association of Anorexia Nervosa and
Associated Disorders (ANAD)**
220 N. Green St.
Chicago, IL 60607
helpline: (630) 577-1330
hello@anad.org
anad.org
ANAD offers a phone helpline, operates a network of support
groups for people with eating disorders and their families,
and provides a list of health care professionals who treat eating
disorders. It organizes national events and local programs and has a
blog and YouTube channel full of information. All ANAD services
are provided free of charge.

National Eating Disorders Association (NEDA)
200 W 41st Street
Suite 1203
New York, NY 10036
helpline: (800) 931-2237
info@nationaleatingdisorders.org
nationaleatingdisorders.org
NEDA is the largest nonprofit organization in the United
States working to prevent eating disorders and provide treatment
information to those suffering from anorexia, bulimia, and binge
eating disorders as well as those concerned with body image and
weight issues. NEDA also provides educational outreach programs
and training for schools and universities.

Project Heal
38-18 West Drive
Douglaston, NY 11363
(833) 365-4325
contact@theprojectheal.org
theprojectheal.org
Founded by two women recovering from anorexia, Project Heal
raises money to help those suffering from eating disorders. It also
works to prevent eating disorders and offers a peer mentorship
program to help those in recovery.

Books

Anderson, Laurie Halse. *Wintergirls*. New York, NY: Viking, 2009.
This young adult fiction novel tells the story of a pair of girls struggling with anorexia—and what happens when one is left behind.

Gay, Roxanne. *Hunger: A Memoir of (My) Body*. New York, NY: HarperCollins Publishers, 2017.
Noted author Roxanne Gay writes intimately about food, bodies, and her own emotional and psychological journey through her struggles with both.

Hornbacher, Marya. *Wasted: A Memoir of Anorexia and Bulimia*. New York, NY: Harper Perennial, 2014.
From hospital stays to loss of jobs, author Marya Hornbacher writes openly about her battles with anorexia and bulimia—and how she won them.

Nelson, Tammy. *What's Eating You? A Workbook for Teens with Anorexia, Bulimia, and other Eating Disorders*. Oakland, CA: New Harbinger Publications, 2008.
This interactive workbook guides readers through their relationship with food, beliefs about food and their body, and more with the aim of helping them overcome disordered eating.

Osgood, Kelly. *How to Disappear Completely*. New York, NY: The Overlook Press, 2013.
A heart-wrenching memoir about disease and recovery, this title examines myths about eating disorders and recovery while the author tells her story.

Websites

Anorexia Nervosa & Related Eating Disorders (ANRED)
anred.com
This website provides information about many kinds of eating disorders, prevention, treatment, and recovery for those who may be suffering from them as well as for their parents.

Eating Disorder Hope
eatingdisorderhope.com
Learn more about the ways those suffering from eating disorders can help themselves through recovery. Relatable and concrete tips, as well as links to other recovery articles, can encourage someone through the tough moments or inspire them to look for further help.

NEDA: 10 Steps to Positive Body Image
nationaleatingdisorders.org/learn/general-information/ten-steps
This area of the NEDA website offers ways people can practice having a better body image.

Proud2BMe
proud2bme.org
This website, written by and for teens, offers a community that promotes positive body image in all aspects of life, including food, exercise, family, and social life.

INDEX

Kristen Rajczak Nelson has written hundreds of books for children and young adults. Her interest in the cause and prevention of eating disorders began many years ago as she observed these behaviors in the running community, and the subject continues to intrigue her as a hobby powerlifter and all-around gym rat. Kristen graduated with a B.A. in English with a journalism minor from Gannon University and an M.A. in Arts Journalism from the S.I. Newhouse School of Public Communications at Syracuse University. She lives outside Buffalo, New York, with her family.